Jesus Lead Me All the Way

Doris Gilbert

Faithful Life Publishers
North Fort Myers, FL

888.720.0950

Jesus Led Me All the Way

Copyright © 2013 Doris Gilbert
ISBN: 978-1-937129-82-8

Published and printed by:
Faithful Life Publishers & Printers
North Fort Myers, FL   33903

888.720.0950

www.FaithfulLifePublishers.com
info@FaithfulLifePublishers.com

Printed in the United States of America.

18 17 16 15 14 13   1 2 3 4 5

THANK YOU and TRIBUTE

- *To my great God, Who has allowed me to serve Him*

- *To Lynn Ramsey, who has so lovingly and capably carried the burden with me, spending hours editing and polishing the manuscript.*

- *To Trish Strickland, who patiently smoothed out multiple rough passages, spending hours in the initial typing and deciphering my efforts.*

- *To Ray Mitchell and Steve Ramsey, who graciously and lovingly took time from their busy schedules to read and correct the many mistakes waiting for their attention.*

- *To the hundreds of people who continue to pray and have anxiously awaited the publication of this book.*

PREFACE

The following poem, a tribute to those who prayed so faithfully, was written one evening, (May 25,1959) to send in a prayer letter.

The road sometimes is long and weary,
>   And often times we feel so afraid:
>   But we face each day with strength renewed
>   BECAUSE YOU PRAYED!

The tam-tams are calling the people to dance
>   The circumcision rites keep up their trade;
>   But we mount up with wings as eagles
>   BECAUSE YOU PRAYED!

We see these dear Christians stumble and fall
>   That we thought would be faithful to the grave
>   But our dismay is turned to faith and hope
>   BECAUSE YOU PRAYED!

Satan keeps telling us that we are wasting our time,
>   Is it worth the price we are paying?
>   Praise God, we can continue to show forth His love
>   BECAUSE YOU ARE PRAYING!

Doris Gilbert

Jesus Led Me All the Way

I met Doris Gilbert on the occasion of her retirement from ministry in France, the last of her multiple overseas missionary assignments. I was witness to her missionary colleagues' affirmation of her. Their respect and affection for her were undeniable. And no group of converts could be more adoring than the university students won to Christ and discipled by Doris. They had come to France from around the world to gain an education. Doris had been the means of their gaining a Savior.

I have now been acquainted with Doris for over two decades. Through every phase of life and in so very many venues she has modeled unwavering confidence in her Savior's superintending influence. She understood when she put her life on the altar as a gift to God that He had sole discretion over disposing of the gift. She never over estimated her right to choose where, when and how she would serve. She never under estimated His right to choose. *Jesus Led Me All The Way* is her declaration of satisfaction in having surrendered to God and having found Him, in all places and at all times, faithful.

Gary L. Anderson, D.D., *President*
Baptist Mid Missions

FOREWORD

For years family and friends from around the world have encouraged me to write a book. My answer has always been, "I'm too busy making history to have time to write it down." The pressure has increased, and after much time in talking to the Lord about it I believe that I have the all-clear signal from Him to try and write this book. Not that I consider my inadequacies adequate, but knowing He is guiding my hand and thoughts, "I can do all things through Him that strengthens me," and "Wisdom comes from Him." Then too, my call went out to my big family around the world for the need of daily prayer partners. Many dear ones promised to "hold the ropes." There are numerous people who repeatedly remind me they are praying faithfully and waiting for this book to be completed. This has been an exciting review of precious fellowship and the day-by-day presence of my Wonderful Lord. My prayer is that you'll see Jesus and honor Him as you read the pages of this book, and see how God lovingly used one of His servants. It would require an entire chapter if I named all who have helped by their encouraging comments and prayers to write this book.

First, they helped with their prayers. Beginning with my parents and many other relatives, hundreds and thousands have prayed throughout the years for me and for the ministries which have been entrusted to me by my loving God. It has been an exciting life and Jesus led me all of the way. Thanks too, to my mother and my aunt, plus another close friend who kept all of the letters I had sent home, and from which I have been able draw upon to write this book.

Second, they helped with their labors of love. There are hundreds or even thousands—only God has the exact count—known and unknown to us. Many have cared and shared with their labors of love. Many ladies' missions groups sewed, others helped pack and ship barrels. My parents and my brothers, Aubrey and Milo, helped in much of the packing and crating, and made sure I had a car to use during furlough. Claude helped by building a rack for the top of the old car as well as many other chores that inspired me. God has all the records, and we are going to see many precious and surprising rewards when we all sit at His feet. Many have kept me on my toes just by asking, "How's the book coming?" Young and old alike through e-mail, Facebook, letters, and in face-to-face discussions ask this question.

Those Who Went Before

In 1607, one of my forefathers, Sir Raleigh Gilbert, the nephew of Sir Walter Raleigh, was awarded a territory in Maine by the queen of England to begin a colony there. My niece and I visited the site and the museum at Popham Colony and Beach. According to the plans laid out for that colony, one of the first buildings was to be a chapel. Even though I haven't found anything to tell me if he or any of the Gilbert family had a relationship with Jesus Christ, the chapel plans indicate that their endeavor was to be one that put God first.

As the story is told, the queen also accorded his father, Sir Humphrey Gilbert, a much larger territory farther north. This included a part of Canada, Newfoundland, and the entire northeast corner of the continent. When he was on the last ship available to return to England after all of the other colonists had abandoned the colony due to starvation and treacherous weather, Sir Humphrey, knowing their ship was in bad shape and likely not able to make the trip, stated, "My life is committed into my Savior's hands." Their ship sank on the voyage home and all perished at sea. Thus, the Popham Colony was never completed because Sir Raleigh Gilbert was called back to England to take care of his father's estate, which included Compton castle, built by his father. This castle still has visiting hours over 600 years later.

In 1630, one of my forefathers on my mother's side by the name of Tillinghast was the first Baptist preacher of the Pilgrim colony at Plymouth. My great-great grandfather, James Friends, gave the land and had much to do in building the West Jackson Baptist Church in Alder Run, near Millerton, PA, around 1876. The church was organized in 1841, and four of the six stained-glass windows have the names of my forefathers engraved on them.

My father used to say that he didn't want to go into the study of the family tree, as he was sure he'd find a lot of dead branches. My family found comfort in the knowledge that no one has written or told them about any robbers or bandits in the family. Maybe that branch of the family travelled too fast, robbing trains on their way to the West Coast, and died in the Gold Rush. Or perhaps they didn't learn to write and thus were unable to jot down any history. Mostly, this history I've just shared is what others have studied and discovered. I am just gluing some of the work of others together to entertain those who come after. Being blessed with this Godly heritage was not sufficient to grant my passage into heaven. No, that isn't the way to Heaven. God's Word, the Bible, says we are all sinners, and we have to personally accept the Savior who died for us. We can't get to heaven on someone else's coattails. Now for the rest of the story . . . .

Her Beginnings

1923

Doris' Birthplace

West Jackson Baptist Church where Doris grew up

The Journey Begins

"Dring, dring." Doris' father cranked the old party telephone ten times from their humble home in the woods, making all the neighbors scurry to their telephones in questioning curiosity: Was it a fire? Are someone's cows out in the road? Did lightning strike a building? Does someone need a doctor? These might have been some of the many questions the whole neighborhood would be asking as they went to listen to the message of the general ring. After hearing a few clicks, the message was clear: "It's a girl! It's a girl, finally," Lee Gilbert yelled over the line. Doris had come to join her three oldest brothers in the Gilbert home.

Years later, a neighbor told her this story of the general ring on the telephone on that day in 1923. Comments were voiced by one and all. Among the opinions was the following: "Lee won't wallop her like he does the boys when they disobey." Boy! That was a very wrong deduction. She got as many whippings as her brothers, and at least half of those she merited. They had a daughter at last.

Her parents were married in 1909, and it was nearly eight years before they had any children. Lee and Nina Gilbert moved with their two oldest sons from Elmira, New York, to a small house built by her great-grandfather Friends. There was no road to it, as it was in a field beside a brook in the woods near the West Jackson Baptist Church. Their third son, Floyd, was born there two years before Doris' arrival. She was born in a rather poor and humble home, nevertheless God's hand was upon each one of their family from the very start, her parents weren't perfect, but their desire was to honor God daily.

When Doris was one year old her parents bought an old house nearby with ten acres of land. Before Doris was two years old her little brother, Claude came to join the family, and it was there where all the children grew up to adulthood. Her parents didn't have the $700.00 to pay cash for the house, so they struggled to pay the mortgage month after month to house their daughter and four sons.

What was this place like where Doris was born? It was definitely in a rural area; the church was called West Jackson Baptist, the two-room school was called Mitchells Mills School, and the whole area was called Alder Run, from the creek which meandered through it with alder bushes along the banks. The first and only Post Office situated on the corner of the road to their house was called Friends.

Before they were married Lee had studied building and business in the University of Pennsylvania in Pittsburgh, helped by his older brother, George, who lived in that area. Thus, he became a builder and contractor all of his life. Nina had already graduated from the Teachers State Normal in Mansfield, Pennsylvania, and taught school before they were married at ages twenty and twenty-one. How could they do all that and still marry so young? I guess kids were smarter back then. They completed their studies in eight years, compared with the twelve years it takes kids these days. It is doubtful most high school seniors could pass the eighth grade exam of those years of which Doris still has a copy.

When she was at the age of the terrible two's, Doris fell off the running board of the car and broke her left arm. She was hospitalized for several weeks. The bone was set wrong, and it had to be reset. Several years later, Aubrey told her that she was a pest and hard to keep in his sights. He was supposed to have been watching her and probably got a licking for not keeping his eye on this terrible two. Giving lickings was part of her dad's daily exercise program. She hadn't been able to use her left arm for several weeks, so everyone was sure she would give up being left-handed and work with her right hand like all normal people. Remember she was only two. You guessed it; that didn't work! She learned early in life to be tenacious.

"We want you to know she is very left-handed, and she will need to learn to write left-handed," her mother told the teacher who always changed lefties to be "normal." That was the practice in all of the schools at the time. Nina didn't give up easily, so the teacher agreed that if Doris held her paper and pencil correctly to write, she would try it and see how well that would work out. "Everybody writes with their right hand, but we can try and see." The Palmer Writing Method was drilled into her head, and in her own stubborn way she became the best writer in the class. Well, what do you expect? The rest were all boys in the first four grades, but they didn't care, so there wasn't much, if any, competition.

Boys, boys, boys! UGH! How would you like to get a dead snake with a love note as a special gift from a boy who has a crush on you? She wasn't impressed. Well, at least, later when she became a missionary in Africa she did not run and scream when she saw a snake, dead or alive. She did have extreme respect for the ones that wiggled, whether it was in the outhouse, in the grass roof over her head, the multiple hiding places in the house where she lived in Africa, or in the grass and paths around it. Whoops! She is getting ahead of herself in this story! That was many years and lots of events before her life in Africa began.

Depression Days and Days and Days

In October 1929, the financial crash came, followed by the Great Depression, and Doris began her "missionary training." They learned which weeds were edible: dandelion greens, milkweed greens, wild leeks, and others. They tapped maple trees and had their own sugar bush to boil down the sap and make syrup to sell and to eat on their pancakes. Apples from the wild apple trees in pastures were made into apple butter to sell to the neighbors. Wild blackberries, strawberries, and raspberries went into jams and fruits for desserts, and all these things along with a big garden helped keep them from starving. They usually had a cow or two and a hand-cranked separator to get cream from the milk to make butter to sell to clients in the city along with the eggs from the chickens. The feed companies made their bags of coarse cotton material with floral designs or other prints expressly so they could be converted into dresses, shirts, and aprons. No one seemed to mind because, "Everyone was doing it."

The churches were full during the depression and revival meetings were held every night. When they finished two weeks in one church they would go to the next church nearby in the circuit for the following two weeks. They were piled into their old car, as many as thirteen people at a time. Car seats weren't in fashion, and neither were they needed, since they were packed in so tightly no one could lose their place. There were very few cars in those days and very few accidents at twenty to twenty-five miles an hour. Of course, it was safer if the brakes were working, too.

No Rights to Heaven

It was during those meetings when Doris was ten years old, that she realized she wasn't ready to go to heaven, even though several of her forefathers and many of her family knew and served the Lord. She learned that "Jesus is the way, the truth and the life, no man cometh unto the Father but by *Me*" (John 14:6). She was born a sinner and needed to confess her sins to be saved. The only right she had was the right to freely accept the pardon from sin offered by God. "The wages of sin is death, but the gift of God is eternal life through Jesus Christ our Lord" (Rom. 6: 23). By accepting that gift she became a child of God. She now had the right to tell others that she was God's child because she had accepted His gift.

Looking back, she realizes how rich she had been all of her life in the things that count, even though they didn't have a lot of material things. For instance, she didn't have her first doll until she was ten years old, but they were taught early in life how blessed they were to have God's Word taught and lived in their own home. As she approached her teenage years, Doris had a very acute inferiority complex. Her parents pretty much followed the fashion of the day, which simply cautioned them not to "praise or compliment your kids much, or they will become proud and haughty." This, of course, wasn't the best method to help them know their self worth. Love was not expressed verbally in their family even though their parents loved them. Expressing special endearments or appreciation just wasn't the thing to do in that era. Being surrounded by boys who loved to tease her didn't build up her self-esteem, either. Whenever she'd complain about the boys teasing her, her mother would say, "They are just teasing you because they like you." Doris never did find a Bible verse to confirm that reasoning. They probably just did it because it worked.

Doris didn't like to answer the phone or go to the door if someone came. She was very anti-social, especially in high school. She avoided putting on her gym clothes in front of the others at school, since she knew the other girls would laugh at the whip marks often found on her body. Nevertheless, she had perfect attendance all twelve years of school. Of course her mother is the one who should have gotten the prize for her tenacity in getting Doris out the door. She was a straight 'A' student for the first ten years, but then with the inferiority complex, naturally, poor grades followed. She had the awful attitude of, "What's the use?" She was made fun of and criticized, which isn't the best way to encourage anyone to study and do better, especially not this stubborn girl. The firm decision was made that she was not going on to college after high school. There would just be more people to make fun of her. Then too, most graduates got married shortly after high school. Not many went on to higher levels of education. After graduating from high school she went to work for a Jewish doctor. She received some serious burns when a gas oven exploded while she was working there. After recuperating, she went to work making typewriters for Remington Rand.

Wars and Rumors of Wars

The draft was mandatory for all young men over eighteen years of age. Most of the boys in her high school graduating class of 1941 went into the armed services, with many of them signing up even before they graduated. The European war was in full swing, and it was that year Japan attacked Pearl Harbor. After church one Sunday morning, December 7, 1941, the family had just returned home and had settled in to listen to the radio. The shocking announcement came on immediately that Japan had declared war on the United States as they bombed Pearl Harbor. Almost instantly, all factories across our country were making materials to help win the war. Remington typewriters were no longer being made. The factory became a war plant almost overnight to make Norden bombsights. No one minded the long hours, and I mean *no one.* Their boys were fighting, and they were doing their part by working long hours in the defense plants and by purchasing US Savings Bonds.

Each piece Doris turned out on the lathe had to be measured for exactness. Only 1/10,000th of an inch of variability was allowed around that tiny piece of brass. For three years six people from their rural area loaded into her dad's car at 6 a.m. to make the trip to the factory. No one had a complaining spirit, even though it would be close to 7 p.m. when they returned every evening. With their boys gone to fight in the wars, those at home were glad they could do their part in furnishing the parts and equipment for the war effort. Many of them didn't have to work on Sundays, but her dad with many others worked seven days a week.

Two of Doris' brothers were already overseas. Both Claude and Milo fought in the invasion of Normandy, the Battle of the Bulge, and other lesser-known battles. Both were wounded and awarded the Purple Heart, but they both came home safe and sound. One more brother Floyd, the father of three children, was on his way to Italy as the war got closer to its end. By this time, no one was exempt, and all the rest of the young men of the area were either already in the service or on their way. Up on the hillside next to the old school house a Community Watch cabin was built, and a telephone was installed. Everyone in the community took their turn to assure a twenty-four hour watch for planes and to report every one that flew over. Passenger planes during the war were practically non-existent, thus any plane flying over was suspicious. Patriotism was the name of the game in every heart and daily program.

His Calling and Preparation, 1944-45

After three years at the defense plant, in the summer of 1944, she was granted a week of vacation. Many years previously she had heard of the LeTourneau Christian Camp, and she had kept a desire in her heart to attend there someday. Even though she had never been able to attend a Christian camp, the Lord reminded her of this hankering when her vacation was granted.

At the camp the first message the speaker shared was based on Romans 12:1-2. God gently showed her through His Word that night that she had spent her young life pleasing herself instead of the Lord by not caring and sharing the message of Christ's love for others. The speaker challenged all of the campers to look at their hands while asking themselves, "Are my hands empty, or have I something to show that I have been working for Him? God's convicting power made it very plain to her that she had "empty hands," and she needed to do something about it. She purposed in her heart to start training and studying to serve the Lord as soon as possible.

LeTourneau Camp roommates

Then came the negative comments from others: "You have only two months. There is no way you can go to Bible school this fall." "Norden isn't going to release you to go to College." "Did you forget there is a war on, and we are making bombsights?" "Did you forget that the jobs are frozen and there is no way to quit?" Upon her request to leave, the superintendent of her department let her know in no uncertain terms, and with language that she wouldn't use herself, that she was working in a war plant. Well, that's that! Oh, really? Before it was time for her to go to Bible school, her department was the only one in that huge factory that was transferred to another city. God is almighty and He arranges everything to fit into His plans. Doris thanked Him for this miracle. Nothing compares to being in business for God.

Within six weeks she was a student at Practical Bible School. "It took a miracle to put the world in space." "I believe in miracles and

I believe in God." "My God is the God of the impossible." It would take more than one book to tell you of the miracles God has wrought by the bushels in her behalf, and He just keeps on caring for this little servant of His. She chose John 3:30 as her life verse: "He must increase, but I must decrease." When she let God direct in her life, she saw more and more of what her God could do.

By God's grace she enjoyed her classes, that is, everything but the study of missions. She could get A's even in Greek, but the missions class didn't interest her that much. She tried to tell the teacher that she didn't understand why. The teacher asked, "Have you prayed about it?" Naturally, the teacher didn't expect an answer. Doris didn't want to get too interested for fear that God might send her somewhere out of the country. Ironically, her roommate was called by the Lord to minister for Him as a missionary in Africa. You guessed it—she received a full menu of missions—morning, noon, and night.

During her senior year, a missionary who was going to start a work for the Lord in Martinique spoke in chapel. At the close of his challenge, the college president said, "You may not be willing to go to the mission field, but would you ask the Lord right now to make you 'willing to be willing.'" Doris thought that was safe enough. You already know what happened, don't you? God spoke to her once she was willing, and she began preparations to go to a pioneer mission field in the West Indies. There was no established evangelical witness in Martinique, and in a few short months she became one of the pioneer missionaries there.

The mission wanted her to do some practical training after she graduated from Bible school in the spring. A few months in the Star of Hope Mission in Paterson, New Jersey, gave her practical insights into sharing the gospel in homes and sharing the salvation message. Women's sewing classes and children's clubs were also means of sharing her love and the message of God's love to so many needy people. Many of these people were either low income or no income people. This followed with a few months training as a practical nurse at Hope Dell Hospital in Passaic County, New Jersey until the end of that year.

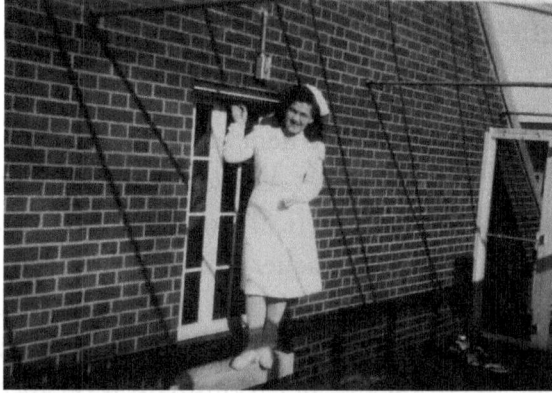

Practical nurses training, Passaic, NJ

In January 1948, the deputation journey began. Support was needed, thus she shared with many churches her burden for the Island of Martinique. "The best support is not from the wallet, but from the heart." Missionaries desperately needed people who would pray for them as they went into the fields to harvest for Him. Romans 10:13 says, "For whosoever shall call upon the name of the Lord shall be saved," but the next verse continues, "How then shall they call on Him in whom they have not believed? And how shall they believe in Him of Whom they have not heard? And how shall they hear without a preacher?" She wasn't a preacher, but she was a messenger to share God's Word to a needy world.

Martinique
1948-51

France
1952-53

Martinique—Here We Come!

In September of that year, with her suitcase, typewriter, and $73 monthly support, she boarded the train in Elmira, NY on her way to New York Harbor. She made a stopover in Binghamton NY to see and say goodbye to her brother Floyd and his family. Floyd was studying for the ministry at the Bible school there. Ida, his wife, told Doris sometime later that as the train pulled out of the station with her on the way to the mission field, Floyd kept repeating the words, "Stay at home and send my sister, stay at home and send my sister." Before Doris came home on her first furlough, Floyd and his family were on their way to the mission field of Brazil.

She had never seen the ocean before. She boarded the French freighter "S.S. Bresle," with French as the only language spoken on board. Very shortly, the crew and twelve passengers realized that she had an invisible sign that read, "Only English spoken here." The captain did know "Jingle Bells," so every evening he met her on deck to sing it with her.

After a very pleasant twelve day boat trip, with ten stops at the islands along the way to unload and load freight, she saw the island of Martinique. It seemed too good to be true. She remained out on deck for hours just praising and thanking God for a safe arrival as they waited to dock. "My Heavenly Father led me all the way," was the song in her heart. She had finally arrived. Little did she realize there would be decades to follow in the service of the King of Kings. Dr. Walter Newman, Arlene Spurlock, and Grace LaMar, all missionaries who had gone on a few months earlier, greeted her at the pier in Fort de France. She was well prepared for whatever the future held for her, right? Far from it! The first of many shocks followed as she had her first introduction to foreign soil.

The following day, the Tetrault family, who were stationed at Ajoupa, a small town to the north of Fort de France, came for her to take her to their station. Heavy rains had made the roads extremely treacherous; the mudslides could surprise them around any curve. It was an unwritten law that drivers had to blow the horn as they went around each curve. After one and a half hours (thirty miles) of reducing exercises riding in a jeep, they finally arrived at the Tetrault's home in Ajoupa Bouillon. Although her body was weary and achy, she was not discouraged, but rather, rejoicing because she knew that Almighty God who had directed her steps thus far was going to give her many opportunities to share the message of salvation with these people. Being raised during the Depression helped prepare her for some of the primitive living conditions. As in her childhood, Philippians 4:19 was still a proven truth from God's Word: "But my God shall supply all your need according to his riches in glory by Christ Jesus."

The Tetrault's home was very small and primitive. Perhaps some would compare it to a shack, with shutters only and no glass on the windows so that when it rained they were closed, which left only kerosene lamps to help break the darkness of the interior of the home. (The Gilberts hadn't had electricity either until Doris was in high school). They had very little of this world's goods, but they were delighted to be there to share the richest message ever told, the message of Jesus and His love to a very needy people. The main need was for spiritual truths. They so needed to hear and know of God's riches and love for them. This was a good introduction to the great need in Martinique.

There were no evangelical churches on the island of Martinique, but there was a small nucleus of Christians where Doris was first stationed, with whom they started meeting in a house in Fort de

France. Also, the missionaries, along with some of the Martiniquans, started covering the island in the jeep and truck over very narrow and winding roads. By doing much of the driving, Doris soon became familiar with the different parts of the motor, as the vehicles would break down often on these trips.

This truck was great to transport evangelistic teams to the villages.

Coming up to a curve, Walter hollered, "Blow your horn, Doris." With steep, narrow roads full of sharp curves, there was no time to ask why. She soon found out that the big trucks carrying bananas or sugar cane came barreling along quite fast over the same roads. Blowing the horn helped somewhat in avoiding accidents. Sometimes they just all stopped in the middle of the road until they could decide which one would have room to pull over if they backed up a bit. The following is an excerpt from one of her prayer letters in 1950:

> "Tonight, I am actually very weary, but I can't put off writing to you in spite of my aching bones. I am the one who does nearly all of the driving, as the other single lady doesn't drive. The director has his hands full with many other activities, and his wife is busy with family duties. We have three or four trips a week into the other communities, and it takes lots of patience, time, and strength to drive over the roads here. There were so many sharp turns with very narrow and rough roads. Needless to say, I am very

thankful to get back safe and sound after a day of hard and dangerous driving.

"Today, I went to St. Pierre and Le Prêcheur with a truck load of workers. I left some off at St. Pierre, and the rest of us traveled on to Le Prêcheur. We go through the streets distributing tracts, and occasionally someone will be interested enough to ask us to explain to them the message, and we praise God once again. Of course, I don't speak to them much yet as my French is quite limited, and my knowledge of Creole is nil. These two towns we visited today are pretty hard, as the people are cold and unconcerned about their souls. It is a hot, deserted area due to the eruption of Mt. Pelée in 1903 when the hot lava flowed down and wiped out everything. Only one person lived through that catastrophe, and he was in a cavernous prison. The deep gorges, which formed the lava beds, still exist.

"We have already started services in some of the communities outside of Fort de France, and more communities are asking for meetings, but we just aren't enough workers to reach everyone. We need men the most. Most of the work that I am doing is really cut out for a man, but when you don't have men you soon adapt yourself, praising God for the part that you can do in sharing the gospel to this very needy land."

The man who was supposed be Doris' tutor of the French language was quite addicted to alcoholic drinks. He was not available very often, as he was drunk most of the time. She always loved kids and was often with them, so she picked up the language by listening to them, and the children were amused and proud to be teaching her French.

The Mechanic at Work

Doris was getting to be quite fluent in learning the parts to the vehicles, as well. She had fixed carburetors, coils, spark plugs, and had cleaned gas lines, besides getting lots of exercise cranking their means of transport to get from point A to point B. The truck and jeep had been a big help in getting the work started in Martinique. Although her mechanical knowledge was limited, sometimes she succeeded in making the necessary repairs to get the vehicles limping back home and to a garage. They often found it necessary to use food money to pay the repair bill when the visits to the garages became too numerous.

The director was a dentist, not really trained for dirty, greasy jobs, thus it was necessary and helpful for Doris to learn as much as possible, which was of course limited. Her entire childhood and youth was spent in training to be a tomboy, not that she had any choice, growing up as she did in a community of boys. Was it worth all of this effort and weariness? Oh, yes. Because of a few faithful workers and lots of prayer warriors, they saw Him blessing the gospel message that they were sharing.

On one of her trips to an out-of-the-way place, she had three flat tires. They were prepared for this possibility, but they wouldn't have chosen the hottest part of the day to remove the tires and perform the necessary surgery (repair them with patches and remount them). Being brought up during the Depression with a bunch of boys had been very good preparation for a lot of things, including putting the jack in the right place so that the car didn't fall down when you took off a tire.

The distribution of the tracts and outdoor meetings, which included lots of singing, gave them many polite listeners and even many who understood the gospel message and prayed to accept Christ as their Savior. As a rule, the people were very superstitious; the sorcerers and the Catholic priests used that superstition to make the folks very leery of the missionaries and their message. Even though the missionaries traveled in groups of mixed color, the locals told the children that white people came to their land to eat them.

Another trip took Doris and the others through torrential rains as they headed for the mountains. One of the things that didn't work too well on the truck was the windshield wipers. The main road wasn't too bad, other than the blinding rains, since those little blades that go back and forth were on strike. Then the mud road welcomed them with open arms and plenty of scares from the one-way traffic.

The journey on foot began with red slippery clay, but they all made it to the top on all fours. The locals made the climb in much better shape than she did. They were only a bit damp, but she was very brown as well as damp. Surely, the locals were snickering, but they tried to be polite and not laugh. With God's hand upon them, they got to the top safely, and there were the people waiting to hear God's Word. Was it worth it?

Farther Along

Doris and her co-worker, Arlene Spurlock, went to live in François, a town near the Atlantic Ocean. They lived upstairs in a house, and the ground floor was set up with benches for meetings. A team would come once a week from Fort de France to do the preaching and have services. Arlene and Doris were there in residence to make one-on-one contacts, to minister to various needs, and to encourage folks to come to the meetings. The people had been told that if they entered the building where they lived they would be cursed. The windows were kept wide open during the services, and although the meeting place was almost empty, the windows would be filled with young and old people listening attentively to the music and message. They didn't come in, but they listened and many accepted Jesus as Savior.

As the missionaries would go to the street corner to get their water from a common spigot, "baby eater" was the main greeting they received as they traveled down the sidewalk. In spite of that, God blessed the witness of His Word because He is God. Many times, especially when she was a bit discouraged and lonely, she would journey to the beach for a walk and enjoy the Atlantic Ocean. As she would see the power of the waves and the vastness of that body of water, she would sing, "The Love of God is greater far than tongue or pen can ever tell; It goes beyond the highest star, and reaches to the lowest hell. The guilty pair bowed down with care, God gave His Son to win. His erring child, He reconciled, and pardoned from his sin."

Rejoicing in His love, she was encouraged to share that message of love with a very needy, sin-sick people. Most of the whites who lived on the island, which was still a colony of France at that time, were there for commercial reasons. The missionaries hadn't come with commercial interest in their hearts; nevertheless, with caring hearts it took time living among the people and sharing the message of God's love from God's Word, for those dear ones to accept the truths they were sharing. In the years that followed, many faithful missionaries continued to evangelize and establish Baptist churches on that island. When they were no longer needed, they journeyed on to share the same message of God's love in other needy lands. Today, the island is covered with pastors, God's servants, and churches carrying on the furtherance of the gospel to their own people.

Father Appreciation

After several weeks of treatment for tuberculosis and complete exhaustion, including a few weeks in a rest home, Doris returned to the United States due to health needs in 1951. During her stay in the Presbyterian hospital in New York City, she was told it wasn't likely that she would be able to continue the same type of ministry due to her extreme fatigue.

When Doris returned from Martinique, even when stopping at gas stations, her father made sure that everyone knew she was his daughter, and that she was a missionary. His approval had not always been the case. Initially, Doris' father had been very much against his only daughter going to the foreign mission field. He told her he wasn't going to give her one red cent to go. He completely mellowed when he realized that she needed to be obedient to God's calling. Upon boarding the train to leave for the field the first time, he put her suitcase on the rack and as he kissed her good bye, he said, "Now if you need anything, be sure and let us know."

He kept that promise until God called him home many years later, at which time Doris was ministering in France among university students. A few months before he died, she was preparing to return to the field. Others, not from her family, declared that she should stay home and care for her Dad. She knew she couldn't do that and be obedient to her heavenly Father, for as she had left for the field the first time God had reminded her of the verse in Luke 9:62, "And Jesus said unto him, No man having put his hand to the plough, and looking back, is fit for the kingdom of heaven." She had learned early in life that the greatest of abilities is dependability.

Amphibian plane that landed twice a week.

The day before her flight, she went to see her dad in the hospital to tell him goodbye. As they prayed together he said, "Father, don't let the words and criticisms of others hinder my daughter from going back to the ministry that You have given her to do for You." God knew Doris needed that encouragement. It was the last time she saw her dad this side of glory, but she knows she will spend eternity with him in Heaven. Although she wasn't able to care for him, he wasn't abandoned because God had given her brothers wonderful wives, and three of the four couples lived near her father. They were all very attentive to his needs, and he graduated to Heaven just a few months later at the age of ninety.

Back on the Deputation Trail and to Regions Beyond

After weeks of rest, Doris was ready to accept the invitations to be the missionary speaker in camps, vacation Bible schools, and mission conferences. It was an enjoyable and delightful time with the children and young people, as she was able to share God's work through her in the island of Martinique. Many of those young people, known and unknown, have served the Lord around the world. As the summer came to a close, she knew the Lord had other plans for future ministry, rather than returning to Martinique.

She had heard much about the need in French Equatorial Africa, and the more she pleaded her case before the Lord, the more she knew that this was the map she needed to follow. She resigned from one mission agency and applied for ministry with Baptist Mid-Missions to go to the dark continent of Africa. During the time she was preparing to meet with the council of Baptist Mid-Missions, she took a semester of post-grad work at Baptist Bible College in Cleveland, Ohio. This school later became Cedarville College. During final exam week in May, she took a long train trip from Cleveland to Waterloo, Iowa to meet with the council. She was the last candidate to arrive. Dr. Ketcham, the president of the General Council of Baptist Churches, was on the council of BMM. She was too tired to be afraid of all of those men as they asked numerous questions: "Give us the ordinances of the Baptist church," Dr Ketcham said.

When she answered, "Baptism and communion," he asked very soberly, "And the third one?"

Not having the slightest clue as to who he was, she said, "Are you pulling my leg?" Needless to say, the ice was broken as those men, with a roaring laugh, broke the tension and fear, and she passed the interview, which was another step in her journey to French Equatorial Africa.

Ship Ahoy

September arrived, and she was on her way to France on the queen of queens, Queen Elizabeth II. She had gone on a twelve passenger freighter to Martinique in 1948; now, in 1952, she was headed for the Northwest coast of France on the largest luxury ocean liner in existence. It was her first exposure to the upper class, according to worldly views. As a child of the King she knew that all of this was temporary, and she was called to share God's riches with very needy people around this sin-sick world.

A New Field: Anyone Here Speak French?

After seeing nothing but water for five days, everyone was excited and pushing to the outside edge of the floating hotel at the cries of, "I see land, I see land," as the liner entered the English Channel advancing towards Cherbourg, France. Upon arrival, Doris was the only one among the group of seven or eight who understood all the questions which were fired at them as their feet touched down in that land she later came to know quite well. Actually, it was time to translate, and everyone needed help at the same time, from English to French and then from French to English for the whole group. Either the custom officers felt sorry for that lady who was trying to keep up with all of the questions coming at her from the French and the Americans, or maybe they were just being kind, because they didn't charge the group anything to get through customs.

The parade to the train station could have easily been called "Yankee Doodle Came to Town," and the people of France were not doing an excellent job of hiding their grins and chuckles as they watched this gawking group, taking in this unknown people, their customs, and their country. After chugging along on the train for at least four hours (the TGV bullet train wasn't in existence yet), they arrived in Paris at Gare St. Lazare. They all were excited and thankful to be met by other American missionaries. Whew! Others could help communicate now.

As Doris already could understand and communicate in the language, instead of living with a French family as was required for new missionaries, she rented a tiny apartment in the suburbs of Paris that other missionaries were vacating as they were going on to Africa. Let's see! The apartment was a seven minute run to the train station, a thirty minute ride to the subway, a fifteen minute ride to the subway exit, followed by a ten minute walk to the language school daily to attend her *moyen* and *supérieure* French classes, which were needed in case she had to teach in French Equatorial Africa.

Tent Meetings in St. Denis

Shortly after she arrived in France for language study, the missionaries who were working in France, Dan and Ida Feryances and Lois Hemmelman, organized tent meetings for twelve consecutive evenings in St. Denis, a suburb of Paris. Each afternoon they had vacation Bible school for the children, many of whom had never seen a Bible before. Six children accepted Jesus as their Savior, and some adults as well, in the evening meetings. Doris was delighted at her first effort in trying to help evangelize France.

As this was shortly after WW II ended, the communists were working hard to influence the people against the United States. Our boys had marched down the Champs Elysses just seven years previously as they helped reclaim France for the Frenchmen. Doris was shocked by the ingratitude of the general public concerning the sacrifices of American lives to help free their country from the Germans. There were signs written all over buildings, "U.S., go home," and pictures of Eisenhower with a hideous grin and each tooth representing an electric chair. Above was written in bold letters, "*He killed two innocent people*," referring to the Rosenbergs, who were spies against the United States during and after the war.

"G.I.'s, Here We Come!"

Doris found more G.I.'s in the Paris area than she did in her home area in Pennsylvania. It was just seven years after "*Victory was declared in Europe on May 8, 1945*," and the G.I.'s were still in the territories where much of the fighting had taken place. Not all the "natives" (especially the communist party) appreciated their presence. However, as she visited in the homes of the French, many were the times that they would weep as they kissed her face and repeatedly say, "Thank-you," for their freedom.

Dan Feryance was able to get permission from the Tabernacle Baptist Church in Paris to hold G.I. meetings every Saturday night. Doris had a friend from Pennsylvania who was stationed near Versailles, and he was "the crier" to announce to the military in that area about the meetings planned especially for them. Everyone was excited, including the missionaries in language study, resident missionaries, and of course the multitude of G.I.'s who were stationed in that area. Special music and help of every kind came from the missionaries, and even some of the military got roped in on ministering, as well.

The dozens and dozens of raised doughnuts that came from Doris' kitchen every Saturday for those special meetings were a big drawing card. She wasn't really competing with the French pastry shops, as the French post-war economy didn't allow for many pastry shops at that time. From the time she was ten years old she had made bread for their big family. This ability, and the opportunity to use it in ministry, became another reason Doris praised the Lord for being raised during the Depression years.

It was exciting to see lives changed, and many of those young men even went into full time ministry for God after their stint in the army. The G.I. meetings ended as well, but it was a profitable and spiritual ministry for those pilgrim missionaries who were journeying through, learning the French language in Paris on their way to many parts of the world. One of the young ladies going to Africa never got there because she became engaged and later married one of the G.I.'s. Doris put her sewing talents to good use and made the first of many wedding dresses. The couple later became missionaries to France, where they labored in the Bordeaux area for many years. Doris lost count of the number of wedding dresses she made over the years and around the world after that initiation. She was no competition with the French couturiers (dressmakers). It was just another ministry the Lord gave her in helping the budgets of young couples who fell in love. Her prices were right, and all was a labor of love and freely given. So that is how she got the job of making wedding dresses. This ministry continued on for many years in Africa as well as France, until her sewing machine retired.

Grateful People

The language studies were nearly finished, and she was able to save enough money to take her one trip to another part of Europe: a trip from Paris to the little country of Luxembourg was on the schedule. She had the desire to visit a family in Luxembourg who had hosted her brother Milo during the war. Some of the fields of battle, including the Battle of the Bulge, were just over the border in Belgium. Milo and other G.I.'s had come from the front lines to rest from battle fatigue in this small village of Dahl in Luxembourg, and all homes in that little country were open to the American troops. Milo had always been welcomed in the same home. This was the family Doris went to visit to thank them. The family was very proud of Milo. They pointed out to Doris where he had sat, slept, eaten, and read his New Testament. Due to their pride in knowing him, Doris was treated and loved as a member of their family.

At the train station and everywhere she went in Luxembourg, everyone she met in that country was so grateful to the United States for liberating their country from the hands of the Germans. She was treated like a queen by one and all. It was very different from the communist influenced country of France. One of the many American cemeteries in Europe is there in Luxembourg, and is well-honored and cared for, even after many years. By His grace, the Lord allowed her to see all of this appreciation for our boys and for our country just before she was to take the plane to journey on to Africa.

The Baptist Church in Martinique today

Violet and Marie Thérèse,
close friends in François

Doris with two cherubs

Street meetings in surrounding villages

Sister Paul who accompanied
me in house to house visits in
Fort de France

Martinique baptism

Central African Republic

1953-72

Giving my testimony on my first Christmas in CAR after six weeks
of Sango language study, before a crowd of 1,500-2,000 people

Good food: The men
killed three hippos
from the Mbomou
river near our homes
for a conference.

Doris and a
sack of peanuts

Head scarves made by ladies
in the United States.

Grapefruit is quite versatile

He hoed weeds to
get his newly printed
Sango Bible.

Children line up for milk from the
dispensary at Bangassou

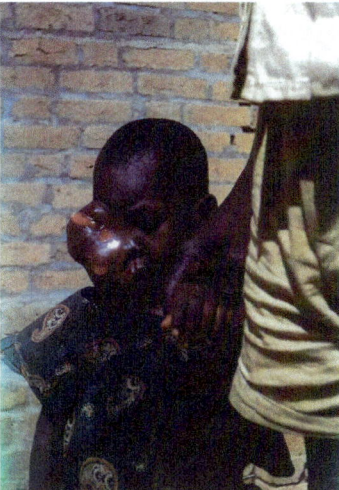

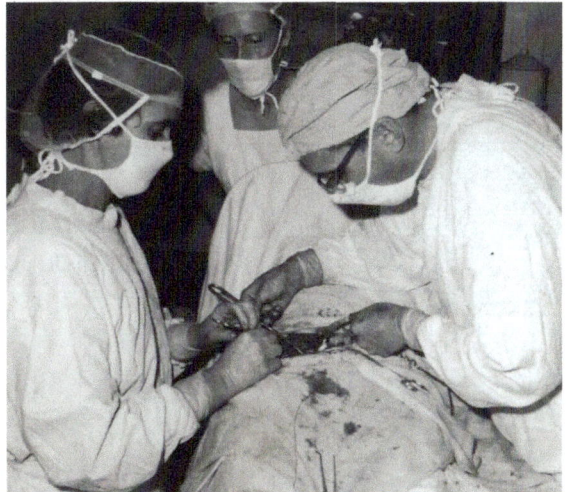

Many cases were very advanced by the time they were brought to
the dispensary. The doctors performing surgery in Bangassou

Doris
and Ruth
Nephew

The girls'
kitchen in
Bangassou

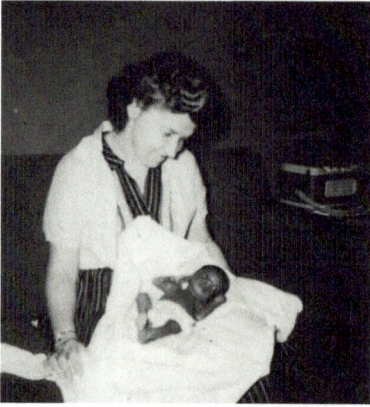

Doris and a
new little one

Nabila and
baby Doris

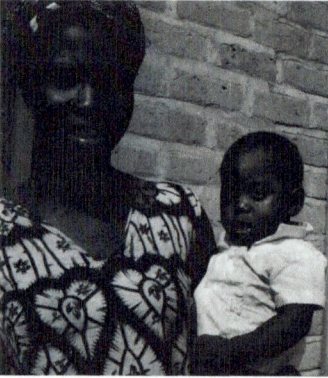

Djiambi and
her son Gilbert

Doris and a
namesake with
her new
house in the
background

Mom and
Lucille-Doris,
October 1988

Lucille,
age 5

Tending Tired Tires

Doris the Mechanic

Trying to change a tire in mud and water

Building a bridge

New roof for Bible school students

"Let's load 'er up, folks." Moving a pastor to an outstation.

Africa Bound

Another continent and another country lay ahead as she left France bound for Africa in 1953. She still didn't know whether she would be teaching in the French school in Fort Archambault (later called Sarh), or if she would be able to go on to do bush work in the Central African Republic, as was her heart's desire. All that area was called French Equatorial Africa at the time, as it was still a colony under French rule. Upon arriving in Bangui, when expressing her desire to do bush work rather than teach, a veteran missionary enlightened her quickly telling her, "We are all teachers." She needed that!

After just a short stay in Bangui, it was time to start up country. From childhood, Doris was well initiated to country, rutty roads and the like; thus, the trip to Fort Sibut, where she was to have lessons in learning the Sango language, wasn't too much of a shock to her.

Adjustments: Language, Food, Hot and Hotter, Bugs and More

Wow! Even though she had spent nearly three years in the West Indies, she thought she had adjusted to the heat but she hadn't seen anything yet. There was plenty of good wholesome food, that is, if one knew how to adjust and adapt to fixing it and eating it. Manioc (cassava) was plentiful, but it was gooey and gluey. The imagination had to be in A-1 condition when trying to make it resemble mashed potatoes. She thought since she liked to cook and bake that surely it would be simple to make a decent and yummy meal.

Let's make some bread. How interesting to find the flour was enriched with wiggly little creatures. They tried to invite them to leave by sifting and sifting the flour repeatedly. It was finally decided they could call it "enriched" bread. Now, about the yeast. No, that packet didn't show any signs of co-operating. Finally, after trying a few packets, there was one that might make the bread rise a bit. The nearest store to find yeast would be in Europe or the United States. That's simple: just write a letter home and send it out on the weekly mail pick-up. Oh well, in three to four weeks they should have some yeast that would make the bread rise. No worries, because they can send yeast in a letter. Just be patient, no phone or computer service. Maybe they could make biscuits while they waited, if they had baking powder or soda that still functioned as it should. Doris enjoyed making pies. Since there were no apples, or berries of any kind, she decided to make them with mangos. They were a bit stringy, but they were eaten up in a hurry anyway.

Doris was expecting snakes and wild animals, but the most pestiferous things were the stinkbugs that got into everything. Everything means everything. They even snuggled down into the loops of tape in the reel-to-reel tape recorder.

Sango was the easiest language she had to learn, as it is based on French phonetics. Of course, she still had to learn the vocabulary, and like any language, there were always some amusing interpretations and thoughts that popped up to give a reason to chuckle. Many of the Sango hymns and gospel songs had fifteen to twenty verses. Which ones to skip when singing a song? None! The dear ones loved to sing, so why would they leave anything out? And it didn't take long for Doris to realize that the Africans could far exceed her in memorization of the Scriptures, even though many of them hadn't yet learned to read.

A Journey of Faith and Service

Christmas in Bangassou, Africa, 1953

Doris' first Christmas in Africa was at Bangassou. Everyone met out under the mango trees in front of Mrs. Becker's grass-roofed mud brick house. She was one of the original five who started the work of Baptist Mid-Missions, with whom Doris lived and learned so much in the few short months before Mrs. Becker left for furlough. The dear ones started gathering at about 5 a.m. in anticipation of the 7 a.m. service. Of course, that didn't stop the early comers (about 1,500 to 2,000 people) from singing gospel songs and hymns as they waited. No need to provide seats for them because they all transported their own stools on their heads. The crowd had doubled by 7 a.m., when the service officially started. Quoting scripture and singing songs, individually and in small groups, made up the program, along with the participation of the entire congregation. Doris gave her testimony, stammering away in the Sango language. They were all very gracious as she stuttered, coughed, and came up for breath; she still wonders how much they understood of what she was trying to say.

Outstation Trip

Just a few days later she went on her first outstation trip. This was one of hundreds she made during her twenty-one years of ministering for Him in Africa. Four of the missionaries went some distance on the river in a dugout canoe, and then walked further inland where 200 people were gathered in an open space awaiting their arrival to give them the Word of God. Very likely, most had been sitting on the log pews or their stools for an hour or two. No one was impatient. Nor were they chaffing at the bit to rush off for the next appointment. They didn't even have calendars, let alone clocks and watches. They had their own program, especially on sunny days, which were quite plentiful in Africa. If it rained, the service or meetings were held later when it stopped, even if it was delayed for several hours. Tired and hungry would quite well express how they all felt before they arrived back at the station. The joy of the Lord was their portion and strength.

Doris was trying hard to learn the language and customs of the people, as three of the ladies were due to go on furlough in a very short time. Mrs. Becker's old, mud brick grass-roofed home where Doris lived didn't have any windows. Double doors opened on to the front and back verandas. Doris slept in the library with its oodles of musty books. Mrs. Becker's books had gotten wet on her initial boat trip to Africa. They were still too good to throw away, and most pages were readable. Doris found the musty smell was a bit overbearing, so at night to make it easier to breathe while she slept, she opened the double doors on to the veranda. That is, she did until one morning Mrs. Becker discovered the open doors. In horror, she quickly informed Doris that the leopards often came onto the verandas at night to look for food. Doris didn't really want to become the leopard's dinner, so she breathed deeply each night and closed the doors.

A Special Privilege Known to Only a Few

Many were the hours Doris sat and listened as Mrs. Becker told of her experiences. Mrs. Becker was one of a group of five missionaries who went to the middle of Africa with Mr. Haas as pioneer missionaries to establish the work of Baptist Mid-Missions in 1920. She had a burden and call to go to the Nzakara tribe. She learned about them from studying in an encyclopedia years before she had arrived in Africa. Bangassou was many miles east of where the pioneer missionaries first stopped to build a work in the Central African Republic. She wrote, "The last restless wait is over," once she arrived at Bangassou, the home of the Nzakara tribe.

Imagine being imprisoned alone in a house in Ouango with no food. Mr. Haas, the founder of Baptist Mid-Missions, had left Mrs. Becker there to minister while he journeyed on to survey the area beyond. In very short order, the Africans, having never seen a white woman, were sure some evil spirit had entered their midst. She told of being locked up in a hut with no food, but little by little she began to see little hands come out of the grasses and bushes, bringing her eggs, fruit, chickens, even bugs and caterpillars, all of which kept her nourished. She would give them money, and that encouraged them to continue to bring her food undercover. During this time of imprisonment she memorized the entire book of Ephesians.

Mrs. Becker told of a so-called road for one hundred and fifty miles of their trek. The following is a quote from *Burning Wicks*, the story of the founding of Baptist Mid-Missions, by Polly Strong:

> "From there they traveled by native paths, walking 'til the blisters on their feet became infected. They then resorted to hammocks. They crossed rivers in dug out canoes; they crossed streams on the backs of Africans, or else they waded. To avoid the heat of the day, they usually started out at two or three in the morning. Africans carried hand torches; missionaries had lanterns. This was more for protection from night creatures such as lions and leopards than for the light. As they pushed through the high grass they were drenched to the skin from the heavy dew and rains.

> "They began to build a work for the Lord on a hill dedicated to devil worship. Mrs. Becker had walked and traveled by canoe all the way inland 495 miles through jungles and in the tropical, hot sun. Many dangers surrounded them as they made the trek of many long weeks."

It was a rich experience for Doris to live with her for six months and learn of their many dangerous experiences and God's protection as they shared God's love with thousands who had never heard. Doris knew that by many standards she herself was experiencing primitive living conditions, but the experiences shared with her by this dear saint were such a helpful challenge and blessing for experiences that awaited her in the future.

The hill where the Bangassou station was established had been originally dedicated to everything connected to demon worship. The witch doctors had tried all of their magic and tricks to get the missionaries off that hill. Our enemy is clever, but our God is all powerful. Needless to say, the devil wasn't eager to give up his territory in a hurry, and it was exciting for the missionaries to see the many people who accepted the message from God.

Not a Dull Moment

With her stammering tongue, Doris started teaching children's classes four hours each morning, plus one Bible school class daily. As mentioned before, when she went to Bangassou, there were three veteran missionaries stationed there who would be leaving for furlough in a few short months. How good to know that many people were praying she could quickly learn the Sango language and stay in good health. Her heart's desire was to be a blessing and to be used of Him, as she was involved many areas of the work that would otherwise have been left without help. She was supposed to take the place of the three ladies teaching women and children's classes, plus teaching in the Bible school, reading classes, and other duties.

Lucille Hukill was Doris' first co-worker in Africa. Doris considered her one of her closest and dearest friends. Although they lived together, their ministries were varied. As one would be coming, the other would be leaving. They rarely saw each other except at most meals and in the evenings. On weekends they both had a burden to minister in the outstations as soon as a vehicle would become available. At that time the church was down the hill near the Mboumou River which separated the Central African Republic from the Belgian Congo. There were about five hundred in attendance for every service. Other ministries connected to the church and the mission were: a four year Bible school with forty-seven students, twenty-two outstations, a dispensary, children's classes four hours daily, women's and reading classes every afternoon, new believers classes, and weekly Bible studies.

Cleanliness is Good, but—

Early in the ministry in CAR Doris found out that one didn't mop the floors, especially when they were made of mud brick. Mrs. Becker's house, where Doris and Lucille continued to live, was in bad shape and needed replacing. The termites didn't want them to feel lonely, so they came to join them in all the walls. The roof was made of grass, mice, bats, lizards, and termites, while the termites and other ants made lots of super highways between the mud bricks.

There were no windows in the dining room, living room, or library, only big openings in the daytime when the double doors in front and back were opened. It was good to know God had a solution, even if it would be many years before a new house became a reality. The real work that God had called her to do for Him was prospering, and she knew that seeing souls come to know Christ would have eternal rewards.

It was not the end of snakes, however. There was often a friendly one waiting on the seat of their outdoor toilet, day or night. Of necessity, Lucille and Doris had to visit the place from time to time even at night. It always gave the feeling that one or more of the snake's relatives might pop up to keep them company. There were many close calls, but God, plus the dear ones praying faithfully were on their side caring for their safety and protection. The bats up in the trees, and the snakes, leopards, and wild cats down at ground level seemed to be delighted to be the source of excitement for one and all.

Back in Business at the Mission Station

All classes started again in February after the students had a month off to go out to the villages to evangelize. With stuttering and stammering tongue Doris started out her day with children's classes all morning, plus time out to go teach the book of Acts in the Bible school for one hour. Reading classes for all adults were in the afternoon. The missionaries wanted the students to learn to read the Word before they were baptized. If they could read the Word themselves it would help them understand for themselves what God was telling them. After baptism classes they would have two hundred to three hundred people each time go down to the river to be baptized.

First Christmas

Soon after Doris arrived in Bangassou, they were invited to Merle and Lorene Watkins' house for Christmas Eve. The girls wore their formal long dresses to help make the occasion more festive. The first course was fruit cup made of native fruits. The menu was sweet potatoes, which grew well in Africa, packaged scalloped potatoes from the States, (white potatoes do not grow in that part of Africa), baked beans from a can that someone had received from the United States, and hand-turned ice cream. Can you imagine freezing enough ice in the freezer compartment of a kerosene refrigerator to make a batch of ice cream? It was often a joint project of all the residents; of course, they all had some of the finished product.

Christmas day, Lucille and Doris had the Watkins family at their house for Christmas dinner, after a three or four hour celebration with their dear African family. Lorene and Merle had received a special gift for Christmas, so they contributed a ham. Doris had cranberry sauce and coffee she had brought from the United States, although it had taken almost a year for her baggage to finally arrive. They finished up the meal with sweet potato pie. It was leftovers for the evening meal, and popcorn for dessert. The latter also had come in Doris' baggage.

The Watkins family became like family for Doris; she loved all of them dearly. She was very blessed to have many precious co-workers, including the couples and their families. The families opened their arms, their hearts, and their homes to her and Lucille, as was the case with the Watkins family. It was a special gift to them from their dear Lord. Being several thousands of miles away from their homes for four years or more at a time, their coworkers' loving care made life so much easier. Doris would count herself especially blessed as she would listen to the accounts of some single ladies stationed in other places, where they felt isolated and very much alone.

The Hunter

Isn't every story in Africa about hunting? Doris didn't take hunting trips, at least not for animals. At Bangassou, the wild animals came to them uninvited; thus they looked for ways to encourage them to leave. They tried hard to make sure that anything edible, including their cats and dogs, were closed into the house each day before nightfall. Not all of the critters were adept at reading the "Not Welcome" signs. One wild cat, or maybe it was one of many, would come up onto the back veranda and make enough of a rumpus to awaken both Lucille and Doris. After several such rude awakenings from their visitor(s), they puzzled over a solution to this problem. Merle Watkins suggested they borrow his .22 Hornet rifle, and await the animal's visit. Sure enough, their visitor arrived. Lucille held the flash light, and Doris pulled the trigger. Got him right in the head, dead shot! Was she proud and thankful? As far as she can remember, she never shot anything again. The girls went out into the rain to pick up the cat, put it in the truck, and take it to the student village that night for the students' next meal.

Lucille, a Dedicated Servant

Every morning, Lucille was at the dispensary to minister to as many as 200 people daily who had gathered on or around the veranda. Many of them needed treatment for parasites and malaria so prevalent in that land. Too often, babies died from the high fevers caused by these diseases. Frequently, patients would be near death when they arrived, due to having been treated by the witch doctors or from trying various African remedies. But, Lucille's main burden was for the spiritual needs of the people. Even before their physical needs were considered, someone was there to preach and share the message of salvation and eternal life to the multitudes present and waiting. God mightily used her caring heart and ministry to win souls to Christ.

Lucille was a dedicated nurse who never hesitated to head out with a lantern or flashlight for the dispensary to answer the call to care for some sick person. As the Africans would bring in sick people from the villages far and near, they would stop on the front veranda of the house where the girls lived. The sick person would groan, and the attendants would yell and pound on the door. It was the custom to believe that the loudness of their groans indicated the severity of the illness. Lucille didn't appreciate the dramatics, and as she would arrive on the scene, she'd kindly say, "You can be quiet now." They would answer, "Yes, Miss," and that was enough to turn off all of the histrionics.

Lucille's dedication and burden to help the people was manifested in many ways. For example, it took her over an hour one night, working with Doris holding a flashlight to remove a filaria worm from a man's eye. Do you know why she didn't wait until the next day? Those dear, tiny worms travel fast and rarely are visible enough to remove, and are extremely painful, but she was able to accomplish the almost impossible task. Back in the '50's, there were six known kinds of filaria. Doris managed to have a close relationship with three kinds. Even for many years after leaving the tropics they continued to show their sincere affection in her body.

How their hearts ached and their eyes manifested their grief for many of the young teenage girls. Often, these girls were circumcised and sold in marriage, suffering illness as a result. One night, a young girl of about fifteen was brought into the dispensary with a very high fever. She had delivered her first child, and had been badly torn because of the initiation process just mentioned. This contamination of her body was extremely gruesome, and was rapidly causing a dangerous and extremely high fever. Real trouble followed, and Lucille patiently worked on her. Doris was there to try to help, although the repulsiveness of the situation caused her to dash outside from time to time to catch a breath of fresh air. Lucille never left the girl's side. After many hours of working with the girl, Lucille was finally encouraged to go back to the house to get some rest. Nevertheless, her heart was heavy for the condition of her patient, and very shortly she was back at the poor girl's side again.

Then, to add to Lucille's already busy life, Doris came down with an acute case of Dengue Fever (often called Break-bone Fever). Although it is not a killer, it makes the one who has it wish that it were fatal. The symptoms are extreme headaches and pain in every bone, and the only solution was to wait for it to go away. No medication helped to ease Doris' pain. Poor Lucille patiently helped her get out of bed, walk, and get dressed. It was at least three months before Doris no longer needed Lucille to tie her shoes. Lucille was much more patient through it all than her patient was. Even though she hurt so that she cried to die, God still had over fifty years of ministry for Doris to do for Him.

Missionaries Had Babies, Too

Dean Chasteen was calling to them down the lane. He came to get Lucille and Doris as his wife Cleo was about to have her third baby. When they got to the house, Cleo, who was busy with housework, informed them that she was fine and didn't expect to have the baby until the next day. The girls stayed, and about 9 p.m. Lucille did a routine pelvic exam and turned to tell Dean that he should go to the government hospital in town and tell the doctor that Cleo was about to deliver, since in cases where there was a government medical facility in the area, they requested that they be advised beforehand, in case of a potential problem. Dean came back shortly, and almost immediately Cleo's water broke. The baby was born at 9:48 p.m., and Doris had the pleasure to care for Cleo and to be present to catch baby Daryl. Lucille, the official nurse, was not expecting such a quick delivery and was busy preparing the equipment for the doctor. He arrived at 10 p.m. to deliver the baby. The doctor scolded Dean for not coming for him sooner; way back in the dark ages of 1954, babies didn't announce in advance the time of their arrival.

Ward Harris came to Bangassou to help in a building project. At the end of the project Lucille and Doris were planning on a buying trip in Bangui, which was a two days trip by truck. This also meant it became a means of transport for Ward to return home to Bangui where he was stationed. Surely that was one of the slowest trips ever taken from Bangassou to Bangui. Ward even suggested that Doris drive part of the time. Have you solved the mystery yet? The truck worked fine, but the love bug had bitten.

A Wedding!

This was an exciting and rare occasion, not only on the Bangassou mission station but among all of the entire missionary population in Central African Republic. Although there was much pressure from the other 'missionaries as to how and where this wedding should take place, Lucille, in her quiet, soft-spoken manner, insisted the ceremony be held at Bangassou, so that the Africans to whom she was ministering could also attend. It was suggested that the wedding should take place at the time of the field conference at Fort Crampel so that all of the missionaries on the field could be present. But Lucille said, "I want my wedding to be a blessing and testimony to these Africans at Bangassou, that they might know that a marriage should be between two people who love the Lord and love each other." Even on the day of the wedding when it was raining so hard that it seemed as though they would not be able to have the wedding outside, some suggested that at least all of the missionaries who had come a great distance could fit into the Watkins' house. Once again, Lucille insisted that it had to be at a time and place where the Africans could be present as well. Yes, their wedding was held outside with about 5,000 in attendance, because the dear Lord had arranged for it to stop raining about an hour before the scheduled time for the wedding.

Were they ever busy getting ready for that wedding! Missionaries came from far and near. Lucille made a lovely wedding dress. Doris had brought two attractive evening gowns back from the United States, and they worked well for her and Mary Sochor, who were Lucille's attendants. Dorothy Rhulman and Mary Baker came from Ndele along with the Farthings. The girls contributed to the music at the wedding with lovely duets.

Much more could be said about the wedding, but it wasn't this spectacular event that made Lucille's ministry so wonderful, but rather her day-by-day living for God's glory and not her own. Due to their burden and love for the Africans, Ward and Lucille's wedding became a great testimony to the people who had never known of Christ's love manifested in such a way. Following this event, nowhere else on the entire field of French Equatorial Africa (this was still the name of that area of Africa before Independence in 1960) were there as many Christian weddings as in the Bangassou area.

The following Sunday, Merle called for testimonies in church. What a thrill for Lucille and Ward to hear how the Lord had used the wedding ceremony to bless so many. It had challenged and blessed many hearts of their dear African family who had never seen a Christian wedding in which the bride had something to say about who she would marry, where the bride and groom manifested their love for each other, and where the ceremony was conducted in a way that glorified the Lord.

It was in stark contrast to the marriage customs of that time when the families arranged the marriages. The custom was to buy and sell brides, and the young girls had no say in the matter. Many times very young girls, even before they reached puberty, were promised in marriage, often times to the highest bidder (they didn't call it that). Or, more often than not, to an older man, or to someone who already had a few wives. The new young wife became the slave not only to her husband, but to all the previous wives.

After the wedding, even though Doris greatly missed Lucille at Bangassou, she was happy for this young couple who had been directed by the Lord to serve Him together. At the field conference, which was shortly after Ward and Lucille's wedding, Doris was asked to go to Bambari to minister there. It was often necessary to reassign missionaries in order to fill the greatest needs. As there were helpers for the children's classes in Bangassou who could carry on the classes there, it seemed that the Lord wanted Doris to go to Bambari for awhile. She eventually returned to Bangassou for another ten years, but more about that later.

First Furlough from Africa

When Doris returned to the United States for her first furlough after four years, she was weary. The first term had included a very heavy schedule of classes, outstation trips, and entertaining missionaries and others traveling through. She was weak from several bouts of malaria, a rough three months with Dengue Fever, and being annoyed constantly by the wiggling worms known as filaria that had come to take up residence, with all of their cousins, all over her body. There were visits to doctors and hospitals for treatment.

Also during that time, Ward and Lucille were stateside as well. They were all looking forward to getting together again at the spring conference. In February, Doris received a phone call from Baptist Mid-Missions informing her that Lucille had been killed in an automobile accident. She had been driving and had hit a patch of ice. Doris stood with the phone in her hand and yelled, "Why? Why? Why?" Her father calmed her down by saying, "Doris, you don't say 'why' to God." What a shock to all who knew Lucille, and especially for her husband, Ward.

Back from Furlough: Faithful Women

Several missionary ladies, all from different regions in the Central African Republic, had the vision and burden to do something special for the women of their churches. Gertrude Morris, Effie Peck, and Doris separately asked for wisdom from the Lord as they made workable plans to start this new ministry. A joint meeting with the ladies was held to discuss ideas and plans.

The Faithful Women were just that. Several times a year area conferences uniting various church groups were planned. Doris would help them organize these conferences in the eastern part of the country, then go to the villages and teach many of the classes. The Africans always gave her the best accommodations that were available, even if it was only a grass mat on the ground. They manifested great love and a thirst to learn more about loving and serving the Lord. The conference would begin at 7 p.m. and go until dark. Bible was the main course, and they ate it up. With such inquisitive minds, they asked many questions and showed a deep interest. Even after they had sat on hard benches or on the ground all day, many times they would ask, "Are we stopping already?"

At one conference, in the middle of a hygiene lesson, a hurried call came from the hut next door, "Madmoiselle, you must come now." Doris suggested that the ladies start singing; then she dashed next door, delivered a baby, and returned to finish her class. Sometimes they would have their babies along the road as they journeyed on foot towards the hospital, market, or even to the conferences. As a result, Doris delivered many babies. She had a variety of experiences since most of the women didn't attend any pre-natal classes. When they had pains they knew it was time to deliver. Much of Doris' ministry was with the women, so that whenever and wherever the pains became quite frequent they would announce that the time had arrived. She delivered some babies in the back of the pick-up, and if the truck was too loaded, they took care of the procedure on the ground beside the truck on the road. Doris always carried a layette or two in the truck, plus the cord, scissors, soap, water, and a sterilizing product. Most of her skills and assistance were needed out in the bush or on the road. As a rule, her help wasn't wanted at a clinic or hospital. With those prevailing conditions there was about a fifty percent mortality of babies at that time.

Road Trip

What was missionary life like? How about a road trip to an outstation? "Come and push, come and push! Miss Gilbert's car died on the way to Bangassou." This was the message that one of the

African pastors sent out on the tam tams. Believers from far and near came to push the truck the two miles back to the mission outstation. Even after Doris had arrived at the pastor's house in the village, people were still coming to help. She was able to get the truck going again, thanks to a huge "how to" repair book that someone had given her, and so they journeyed on.

Nakaba, a woman from Bangassou who had only one leg, and a young dwarf were traveling back with Doris from a Faithful Women's conference at Bakouma. They had traveled over rocky roads and rotten bridges. As they were crossing a river onto a ferry that never seemed to get close enough to the edge of the road on the other side, the rear tires dangled in the water. Just as Doris drove up the grade from the river, a young woman stopped them to ask for a ride, and the motor stalled. The battery was dead because they had been traveling many miles with a defective generator. People gathered and pushed again until it started, and they were on their way again with one more passenger.

They stopped at another outstation to greet the pastor and his wife before continuing their journey. "Why don't you stay with us tonight?" they asked. Doris and her crew were weary enough to be tempted to accept their offer. They had already pushed the truck three or four times that day; however, Doris was concerned that the folks at Bangassou would be worried, so they journeyed on. Two miles farther the truck declared that it was too tired to journey on, so once again Doris sent word to the pastor and people that they needed a push. While waiting there beside the road, a truck came along with three fellows in it. It was an opportunity to send a note to the folks at Bangassou to relieve their minds. By that time it was dark, and without a battery or generator they had no lights. The folks had arrived and had started pushing the truck with one man running ahead with a little kerosene lantern. This might be called an old story, but the dear people sang while they pushed the truck through the dark, as if this were the greatest privilege that they had experienced in their lifetime.

Doris was so weary by the time that they arrived back at the pastor's house and parked the truck. She had taught the women that morning from 7 a.m. until noon before they had started their journey. The pastor's wife told her that Mrs. Becker had taught her how to massage backs. Do you want to guess what Doris said when the offer came to do hers? The leader of the Faithful Women's group offered to give her a bath, but she thought she had enough energy left to manage that by herself. After reading and praying with the others, Doris had water and bananas for her supper before going to bed. The Africans always give their best and that was what they had. A typical African bed was made of bamboo slats in the form of a hammock, with the feet and head in the air, making it conducive to curvature of the spine. There was no mattress and no sheets, but the pastor's wife had some dress material that served the purpose. Doris "slept" until dawn.

After morning devotions, she had breakfast. Bananas and water were again on the menu. Doris took the generator off the truck and started to clean it. It took two hours just to clean off all of the dirt, grass, and mud. She changed the points and got everything back together and mounted in place. With a little shove the truck started up about 10:00 a.m. After eating bananas and peanuts, they were once again headed for Bangassou.

Six miles down the road the truck protested, "I don't want to climb that hill." This time Doris blew out the gas line, checked the fuel pump, changed the coil, cleaned the spark plugs, and filed the points. They were on their way again, but the old dear truck seemed to sing the same refrain, "I want to rest, I want to rest..." They were now too far from even an outstation. They threw the tarp on the ground to sit on and to discuss what the next step was to be. Doris wrote another note to send to the mission station at Bangassou in case another vehicle should come along. She had just folded the note when a Frenchman driving a Land Rover stopped to help them. He said that he would deliver the note immediately upon arriving in Bangassou. Coincidence? That was the only vehicle that passed that day heading toward Bangassou. God had promised that He would never leave His children or forsake them. They sang, read God's Word, prayed, and witnessed to the folks passing by, as well as to the young lady they had picked up at the ferry. They had some bananas to eat and water to drink, and waited there for six hours.

By 3:30 p.m. an African pastor and a group of people had gathered. Someone asked, "Why did this truck have to do this to you?" Doris replied, "It said, I have worked very hard and I want to rest." Of course, the main reason was that there were many people who heard how to be saved because of the multiple stops and starts. Once again, over hill and dale the truck was African- propelled back to the nearest village because the pastor refused to allow them stay on the side of the road all night. They left the truck at the home of an African believer in the nearest village.

The next mode of transportation was a bike. The man's bike that they brought for Doris was incompatible with her short stature. A ladies' bike was found which worked well as long as she didn't sit down. But as soon as she sat down the rubber didn't hit the road because she couldn't reach the pedals that way either. By this time many of the by-standers concluded that she must be short or that her legs weren't very long. A solution was found when they lowered the seat.

Riding over the rocky roads with a bike made her realize how comfortable her truck had been. The rubber was missing on one pedal and the front wheel was a bit loose. She eventually covered the five miles, huffing and puffing most of the way. It would have been easier walking, but one has to be careful about refusing generous offers. Nakaba rode on the back of the pastor's bike, and the dwarf came along behind. It was dark by the time they arrived at the pastor's house.

Doris' clothes were soaked with perspiration, and her hair was dripping wet. She developed a lingering rash from wearing her hat for so many hours. After a bath, she ate bananas, peanuts, and chicken that the pastor's wife had fixed in palm oil. She said a missionary named Merle Watkins had taught her how to fix chicken *bounjou* (white-man) style. Doris had just finished eating when she heard Bob Golike's truck coming from Bangassou. The Frenchman had gone directly to the mission station, but it had been quite dark when he arrived. Bob was an excellent mechanic, but since it was already dark it was deemed wiser to continue on to Bangassou and return the next day to fix the truck. Incidentally, the first note they had sent never did arrive.

By the time the truck was ready the next day, the passenger list had increased by two women with a child who had been sick for five months. The child died the next day, as often it was the custom of the Africans to wait too long to seek medical help from the missionaries. They were saddened to tears many times upon seeing the people that had come for help too late. A man also asked Bob for a ride and insisted that he didn't have any baggage. In reality, he had two big baskets of dried meat, and he had invited a friend to go along. While loading the truck, they proceeded to tie their two bikes to the sides of Bob's truck without asking permission, of course. After many such experiences the missionaries became accustomed to the Africans "very little baggage" when they asked for a ride.

After lunch the next day, they went back to the mission station for battery cables. They also took parts and chains in hopes that something would help them get Doris' truck back on the road. Well! What was wrong? There was dirt in the jets of the carburetor!!! Doris had taken the thing apart, but all she had learned about engines, she had learned from experience. She always carried the big Chevrolet shop manual in her truck, and that helped some. She had never previously had jet problems; at least she would know the next time.

With a little boost from Bob's battery they were soon on their way and in good shape, she thought, until upon arrival she found that they had a broken rear shock. That was the third one that year. The truck used extra gas, as they had to travel in lower gears due to lack of power. There were no gas stations on the way, but they always carried a fifty-five gallon drum of that liquid stuff on the back of their pick-up along with the usual extra passengers.

You might be wondering why they would go through all of those problems to go to a conference at an outstation. If you could have heard the women testify and praise God for the lessons they learned those few days of how to live to please God, you would agree with the missionaries that it was worth all the energy spent going over those rough roads, crossing the river on the ferry, and experiencing the fatigue and hardships to be able to teach the wonderful Word of God to those dear ladies. God worked in their midst, and Doris was certain that it was a direct answer to the prayers of many dear Christians around the world. Ironically, that Sunday morning Doris had told the ladies that the trials were to refine them. Well, they got some chiseling, not just refining. Not all of their trips were like this one. Not more than fifty percent, to be sure. As the song states, "It will be worth it all when we see Jesus." They had read enough missionary stories and listened to the first-hand accounts of the senior missionaries, so that the surprise wasn't too great. Many precious promises from God's Word helped keep their hearts happy and confident that their Heavenly Father was directing their paths, just like the Bible tells us, "In all thy ways acknowledge Him and He shall direct thy paths" (Proverbs 3:6).

Grocery Shopping in the Belgian Congo

From time to time, Merle and Lorene would cross the Mboumou River that separated the Central African Republic from the former Belgian Congo. Bangassou, where their mission station was located, was right next to the river. The ferry, which was made up of dugout canoes, would take them across. Then it was another day's journey to some small stores. Over in the Belgian Congo, before their independence in 1960, many things from Europe were available that could not be bought in the Central African Republic. The Watkins often shared something from their trip with the girls. Probably the most exciting gift that they brought back to them was a can of hot dogs, for they hadn't seen any of those in many months. Bangassou had a couple of shops where they could buy food staples such as rock salt, rice, and beans. They could also find some canned goods occasionally, but very often they were rusted through.

They went in to town mainly to buy kerosene and gasoline. The gasoline was for the vehicles, but the kerosene was for their refrigerator and lamps. The kerosene refrigerator, like everyone had, came equipped with a big pan at the bottom of the fridge, which if they kept it filled with kerosene and the wick trimmed, they could usually convince the refrigerator to produce some ice, and cool off the water that they had boiled for twenty minutes and then filtered. The refrigerator didn't always function properly, and that usually was because they weren't very adept at caring for it. At other times it co-operated so well that it made enough ice for them to use their elbow grease to turn the old freezer and make ice cream. This is what they considered "living it up." Since all the missionaries cooperated in making and contributing the ice in from refrigerators, they were assured of having their part in the feast.

Cooking with Charcoal

Charcoal was the main fuel for cooking, boiling water, and even baking. Their kiln was made of bricks and built up to counter height. With a hole in the front and one on top, the air was able to circulate.

They would put the charcoal inside on the rack, and once it was hot enough with live coals the operations began. It was much like any other oven. One soon learned how much time was required to build up the heat needed, and to bake a loaf of bread. Lightweight aluminum pans did not last long in those conditions, so they used cast iron. The large kilns were also used for roasting goats or baking chickens. Only a few short months later, they were using a portable tin oven over a charcoal fire. One learned to be vigilant, or plan on having a burnt offering. They also used an open temporary oven built with a few bricks to cook their goat meat. They had many good laughs trying out and learning the different methods of preparing food.

The abundance of fresh fruit was a real blessing when the menus didn't turn out exactly as planned. It was always advisable to follow the exhortation from the Scripture in Ephesians 5:18, "In everything give thanks: for this is the will of God in Christ Jesus concerning you." They really did try hard to have happy and thankful hearts, recognizing that but for the grace of God, they would still be slaves to Satan, and that God had given them a high and holy calling.

A Fruitful Field

Shortly after arriving in Bangassou, Doris began teaching classes in the Bible school, children's classes five mornings a week, and baptism and reading classes in the afternoons. As often as possible, they would journey to the outstation villages around them on weekends. Doris considered it a real privilege and honor to be a messenger of the gospel of Christ in spite of scorpion bites, tropical ulcers and sores, malaria, filaria, and dengue fever.

In many unreached villages, the people were very superstitious, and engaged in demon and Satan worship. The missionaries had God's Word to share, the only message of salvation that could set them free. The Central African Republic was the most receptive field to God's truth of those in which Doris had ministered. It was not uncommon to have close to a hundred people standing beside a muddy, germ-infested pool to be baptized, even though they were well aware of the risks from schistosomiasis, a parasitic worm common to the tropical waters.

Merle had written "A Day with the Watkins Family at Bangassou" shortly after they arrived, which captured the sense of a typical day:

"The stillness of the African night is broken by the deep bass tone of the station tam tam as it announces that a new day is dawning, and since we didn't get home from a bush trip until 11 p.m. last night, we would have enjoyed another hour or two of sleep. The Africans are already milling around waiting for the morning prayer meeting to begin. We slid out from under the nets dressed, and twelve minutes later we were at the children's chapel for prayer meeting. The station work crew, a few deacons, and several women have gathered to render praise and speak their petitions to the Great Chief. The language would be strange to many reading this, but our God understands all languages. As the sun peeks over the palm tree we know it's time to close in prayer. The work is assigned for the gardeners, water men, and brick crew. Now it is time for breakfast. Maybe rice, maybe rice and peanuts, peanuts with rice, or rice with peanut butter. Often we have peanut butter with bananas, too. Family devotions follow breakfast, seeking directions and blessings as we serve our Wonderful Lord.

"At 7 a.m., it is time for the first class at Bible school, which will continue until 11:30. Loreen is having class with the children. If you take a peek you will see 250-300 black-skinned kiddies sitting on rough benches, busily engaged in learning to read, write, memorize scripture, or listen eagerly to a Bible story.

"The sun has been beating down since 8 a.m., and the shade of our new house is so welcome and refreshing. A nice cool shower is a good picker-upper and the fried hippo steak smells great. "Come and eat" is the signal for all of the family to head for the table. We thank Him for the good morning and for the food. French-fried manioc, spinach greens, and homemade bread await us. We finished off the meal with a nice big juicy slice of pineapple, which is grown locally.

"Siesta time for one and all! It is very hot and sleep comes quickly, but so does the booming of the tams tams. It was time for all activities to start again. Roll call again for the men who will be cutting trees for the new houses that we are building for the sick people that live long distances and cannot return home every day. Classes begin at 2 p.m. and run until 5 p.m. They vary from day to day. Every day there are reading classes for men and women, children's classes, and church members' classes. New convert classes are on Wednesday and hygiene classes Tuesday and Thursday. Prayer meeting for one and all is on Wednesday evening, with no classes on Saturday. Prayer meeting was at 5 p.m. that day. There are other things to do and supervise when we are not in the classroom. Even classes get interrupted from time to time to kill a poisonous snake or some other varmint.

"The big drum booms at 5 p.m. to signal the close of the work hours. The Africans are everywhere, singing gospel songs and choruses as they head for their villages. Soon it is suppertime, and the little light generator is turned on and the family gathers around the table. Antelope soup tonight. We thank our Lord once again for His faithfulness to us all day. The evening is used to prepare the next day's classes, write letters, and play games if we aren't called out to get a sick person, or to treat someone with a high fever or other illness. It is all in a day's work, and we once again rejoice that we are called to serve Him in Africa."

Doris' First Missionary Conference in Africa

A two-day trip over rocky and rough roads took the missionaries to Fort Crampel. In the early years there would be about 150 present, including the families. It was the event of the year for one and all. They made new clothes, and often the lady of the home would make dresses and shirts of the same material so that all of the family could be dressed alike. This was the opportunity to enjoy skits, special music, and most of all, fellowship that they longed for from being separated from one another by at least a day's journey during the rest of the year. Before the conference, Doris made dresses alike for the four ladies on the station. They also had a swap shop at conference, and much of their Christmas shopping was taken care of then. One person's surplus can be someone else's treasure.

Why Crampel? That was where the missionary children's school was located; thus, they had a dormitory, which also meant extra rooms and extra beds. Some of the single ladies slept in storerooms, on multiple cots in someone's living room, or in the corner of some other room roped off for privacy with a blanket or quilt. They were just missionaries, and didn't expect luxury accommodations.

At this conference, Doris was asked to transfer from Bangassou to Bambari. The requests had gone in from three stations, including a return to Bangassou. It was decided that the greatest need was at Bambari.

Many Hats

Doris went to work at Bambari along with the Teachouts and the Halls. Among other things, she ministered five mornings a week to about 150 children. Their ages varied from five years old to sixteen. The older boys weren't sure that they needed to follow her directions, and acted like typical teenagers. When she requested that everyone sit down, one of the boys remained standing to let everyone know that he didn't have to do what Doris told him to do. She slowly went to where he was standing and asked him if there was a reason that he didn't follow orders. He was at least a head taller than she was, but she used her knee at a certain angle behind his knee, and he sat down. Of course this was followed by chuckles from the other kids. That was all it took to limit the discipline problems. She was there for God, and He continually gave her wisdom for situations for which she didn't normally possess.

Teaching, writing, and translating lessons, as well as programs into the Sango language, cooking meals, and entertaining for the many that needed motel accommodations were all part of the ministry. Also, Doris had her back-door clinic where she cared for all sorts of medical needs, anything and everything. There were cuts, ulcers that required months of daily care, strep throat, chicken pox, miscarriages, and high fevers from malaria which especially affected babies. The local French hospital kept Doris supplied with malaria medicine for the babies. Their fevers seemed to be especially high in the middle of the night. She knew when she heard the clapping of hands near her bedroom window that someone was in need of help. Occasionally, she needed to go to the student village to care for someone who was too ill and weak to come to her house. With no dispensary on the Bambari station to turn to, Doris did what she could to help the sick from her back door.

Bambari is located at a crossroad and was also the midway point for many of the missionaries traveling from their stations to the missionary children's school, or to the capital city of Bangui. Then too, conference was held each year at Crampel where the children went to school. The missionaries at Bambari needed to get bread baked, prepare lots of food in advance, and boil many gallons of water over the charcoal fires for at least thirty-eight overnight guests who would pass through on their way to conference. All would want to take showers to rid themselves of the deep "tans" that they had acquired from the dusty roads during their journey. The shower bucket needed to be filled many times, as they needed to have the empty shipping barrels filled in advance to make sure that they didn't run short of water, and could be heated by the sun. As many, if not more, would be coming back that way after conference. Several would bring their children back for their vacation from school at that time, increasing the numbers. The missionaries always managed to find sleeping arrangements and food for one and all. Showing hospitality to God's dear ones was a welcomed ministry at these crossroads.

Another ministry Doris had was teaching. The children's class each morning required lots of time and strength, but was such a delight. In just a few short months after arriving at Bambari, Doris had the privilege and joy of seeing over sixty children accept the Lord Jesus as their Savior. In each prayer letter that she sent to the United States, she pleaded with her prayer partners to pray for the children. It was evident that they had open hearts and minds to the gospel message. They loved to sing, and were adept at memorizing Scripture, and because they also were willing performers, Doris wrote a complete program called "Living Water" for them to present at the main church service. It would have thrilled your hearts, as it did the missionaries', if you could have heard them telling others of what Christ had done for them, and challenging the audience to come and drink of the "Living Water." The children led the entire program. The master of ceremonies, the song leader, and those giving object lessons with messages, doing the acrostics, and telling the creation story, were all children. One little girl's father accepted Jesus, "the Living Water," that morning. Many were the programs for special occasions that Doris wrote and helped the children produce. It was as much of a blessing for her to see their enthusiasm as it was for the children to faithfully prepare and share the message.

Over 150 children regularly attended Doris' class. There were some children who had the privilege of being in French school during the week. They faithfully attended the classes on the station on Saturday morning. Germain, one the more faithful ones, later went on to become a pediatrician in Bordeaux, France. Imagine the delight awaiting Doris when several years later she was directed of the Lord to go to Bordeaux to minister among the university students, and their paths crossed again. She had the joy of "setting in" when Germain defended his thesis to become a doctor.

Bible School and Seminary

While they were building the seminary classroom and housing for students, they needed to haul a lot of sand, gravel, and stones from the nearby creeks and other places. Doris passed the test to drive the truck so that she could help with the trucking when she wasn't in class. As long as she had a physical exam every year, the permit to drive the truck remained good.

Not all were happy moments. During one of the trips to the river, one of the Bible school students decided to dive into the river. The missionaries never found out whether a hippo or some other animal got him, or whether he had gotten into deeper water than he could manage. He was never seen again. This caused much deep sorrow, along with frustration, as many of the Christians thought that the missionaries should take several trips with the truck to take them all to go to the memorial service held that same day, involving a two hour trip each way. As in any other country, when there is sorrowing, not every situation gets a correct answer. This sad experience was the cause of much misunderstanding and heartache for God's work. The missionaries needed much wisdom and direction daily to do God's work God's way.

When they were about to open the seminary, Paul and Vivian Beals and their family arrived to work at the station at Bambari. Doris enjoyed this family, and the children often came to see her when they weren't at boarding school in Crampel. When his older brother and sister were away at school, Sammy was at her house as often as his parents would let him. One evening about suppertime, he said, "Aunt Doris, could you invite me to supper? My mom said that I had to wait until you invite me." So with a chuckle, she said, "Sammy, would you please ask your mom if you could stay for supper?" She enjoyed all of the children immensely, no matter what their color or nationality.

Recess was always part of the morning program for the children. They were not familiar with the game of baseball. Doris decided with a hundred and fifty kids in class there should be enough for two teams (yes, she knew it only took nine for each team). She proceeded to engage them in playing baseball to give them a bit of added variety. She had some old curtains that were stained, and she decided that with a little dye that she had solicited from family or friends (ladies groups often requested a list of her needs), she could have two teams, red and blue. Sometimes she laughed so hard that she had a difficult time explaining the game: "You mean you have to touch the runner with the ball, not just throw it at him?" "Why do we have to run to first then second? Why can't we run straight across to second base? It would save time." It is doubtful that they really learned the game of baseball, but nevertheless they still talk about it fifty years later. Germain, the pediatrician in Bordeaux, mentioned it again when Doris made a recent visit to Bordeaux.

Doris' Hair Salon

Another one of Doris' ministries was hairdressing. Throughout her younger life, she gave permanents to her mother, aunts, and sisters-in-law, and set their hair each week. Later, while she was in

Bible school, every Friday and Saturday her hairdressing occupation thrived at fifty cents a head. Then, as a missionary in Africa, her services were once again much sought after. On one occasion, when conference was just around the corner, many needed to have permanents and haircuts for the big event. Her dear co-worker at Bambari, Linda Seymour, was one of the first clients that time around, with the following list of requirements for her pretty white hair: "I want you to cut it short, but not too short. Watch the hair by my ears, as it is pretty thin, and get rid of as many dark hairs as you can. I don't want my hair to be fuzzy, but I want it good and tight. I don't want to look skinned though. I want it long enough to roll on the rollers so that those that might object won't know that it is cut. I want it to last a year this time and not grow too fast." Doris didn't give any guarantees. Nevertheless, Linda was very pleased with the results; she really wasn't as hard to please as it sounded.

Some of the other missionaries came early from other stations in order to get their haircuts and perms, too. Even when their hairstyles needed attention and it wasn't at the time of the yearly conference, some would make the two-day journey, bearing their Toni or Lilt home perms, to get the service of their favorite and only hairdresser.

Later, while working at Bambari, Doris took a trip to Bangassou to visit the dear people there where she had first ministered in Africa. There was always a loving welcome by one and all. Besides spending hours greeting them all and praying with many, she helped beautify the station by doing a couple of permanents. One was quite simple to do as it had the directions, but Elda Long had brought a professional type perm to the field with no directions. It was one might call a "guesstimation" process, and they must have missed a step because Elda's hair turned out quite nicely, but Doris' hands burned with extreme pain for at least two days. She also lost all of her fingernails causing extreme discomfort for some time. She said, "All in a day's work and a month of pain."

In Africa, Doris also did a fair amount of sewing. There were no department stores, such as Penney's or Woolworth's. She made dresses for herself and several others ladies and girls, as well as shirts for some of the men and boys. One day while she was sewing, her houseboy asked her if she ever rested. She told him that she had fun serving others; this was true all of her life.

Ministering to a Dear Friend

Lorene Watkins, a dear friend from Bangassou, fell deathly ill while staying with Doris. The Watkins' had come back from the mission hospital at Ippy, since Lorene was having problems with her pregnancy. Dr. Fisher wanted the opinion of the doctor at Bambari, and the doctor there didn't deem it wise to move Lorene again. Doris went to Ippy, taking Lukie Watkins, her two-year-old assistant, and packed up all of the Watkins' things to bring them to Bambari. The plan was to operate the next day to remove the baby that had been dead for some time in her womb. As the doctors were doing the surgery, they discovered not just one, but two baby girls. Lorene had hemorrhaged badly, and she had already received two transfusions, so they deemed it necessary to take her back into the operating room to remove the uterus and give her another transfusion. They all feared that she wouldn't make it as she had stopped breathing several times during the procedure. They almost lost her, but she did recover. It was a long road for her to get back on her feet. The Africans and Americans were praying much for Lorene, their dear sister in Christ, but God saw fit to spare her life.

Mary Sochor stayed at the hospital with her, and the missionaries took meals to them each day. Doris took care of meals for Merle and for little Lukie. Later on, Lorene stayed with Doris for a couple of weeks to try and get some of her strength back. She especially needed encouragement and counsel from God's Word because she kept saying that it was her fault that the babies had died. Besides the care of Lorene, Doris tried to keep up with Lukie, the Watkins little fellow that was two years old at that time. He helped keep Doris entertained and busy, and he was cute as a button. While Lorene stayed with Doris after she got out of the hospital, Merle, Lorene's husband, went to Bangui for business. Although Lorene was still quite weak when he returned, she was eager to get back home to Bangassou. This was another long day's trip over rough and treacherous roads, but God spared their dear sister, Lorene.

Filariasis

Linda Seymour and Doris were taking turns having swellings in their arms, hands, and other parts of the body, caused by a sort of wee little insect that would manifest its importance by injecting the larvae from an infected person into another person. This resulted in blood sucking worms that did a lot of crawling all over the body. The females measuring from one inch to twenty inches produce thousands of micro filaria that travel from spot to spot in the body. Localized edema, accumulated fluid, causes swelling all over the body. One type causes blindness; another type travels just under the skin. These Doris picked out of her fingers, hands, and feet by the hundreds. This can develop into elephantiasis, and many Africans were afflicted with enormous limbs that could not be reduced in size.

In a letter to her parents she attempted to define filaria: "Now for the story of the worms. Once upon a time a little insect was flying around and he decided to light upon a young lady who had never done him any harm. With his little hypo needle, he injected some serum that caused little worms to crawl and crawl in the young lady's blood and flesh. Day and night, they traveled all over, exploring new territories, discovering new dwelling places, until she decided to wage war. She sighted the enemies and dropped bombs of pills named notezine. Needless to say, it was hard to guess which side would come forth victorious as both sides were fighting a terrific battle. The entire area of combat began to look like a battlefield that was worn and torn. One by one this strong ammunition eliminated the little worms. The jury is still out as to which is the worse, the malady or the medicine. Some of the enemy troops had been slain or were at least declaring a truce. The battle had been going on for eight days already, but she still needed to take two more days of treatment. Both sides rested for ten days, and then the battle started all over again to be finished hopefully in ten days with notezine the conqueror. This was not the end of the story of the worms. The babies would soon become adults, and the drama would start all over again. It should, however, give a reprieve to the young lady for a time."

Doris became the prize patient at the Guthrie clinic in Sayre, Pennsylvania, on one furlough, when she was hospitalized for a routine procedure. At the same time, she gave the doctors permission to experiment on some of the swellings the doctors found on her body. The patient was hospitalized for other reasons, but they didn't often get opportunities to treat filaria. Doris later found a hospital report from Guthrie clinic, which showed that they did succeed in finding and reporting on two kinds.

The treatment to quiet down their activities in the body is quite severe and often Doris, and many others were obliged to completely stop all activities during the treatment, which lasted for at least three weeks. There was no known cure, but supposedly they go to sleep after ten years away from the tropics. Even though she left the tropics over forty years ago, Doris wonders sometimes if some of the itching and rashes she experiences are not from the little worms waking up from their naps.

Penny Becomes Part of the Family

After a bit of effort convincing Linda that it would be helpful, Doris acquired a dog. He was part German shepherd and part Golden retriever. Ben Kendrick told Doris that she should call him Benny after him, but eventually it became Penny. Doris often said jokingly, "Penny, because he isn't worth two cents." She really didn't feel that way about him, though. He was a great companion and almost a watchdog, if he didn't decide that you would make a good friend. The African kids, as well as the missionaries' kids thought he was great.

Since none of the village animals were fenced in, they were often on the verandas and in the house if the door was left open. Penny was vigilant and helped escort the unwanted animals, including two-legged thieves, away from the house. The pots and pans used for cooking and boiling water on the charcoal burners were kept outside on the veranda, along with much of their food. For a people who had very little, seeing these pots big and little were a temptation for passersby. All the cooking, washing, and ironing (with charcoal irons) were done on the veranda. Not only was it dirty, but also inconvenient when the winds and storms decided to visit. Teakettles, dishpans, ironing board, and iron often walked away if they didn't blow away first. After they got Penny, not as many things disappeared. Incidentally, the dog didn't terrorize the storms.

Penny was a great help and protection. One time he almost died, and they suspected that he was poisoned. He had been alright on Saturday night, but by the next morning he was vomiting and completely without strength even to stand. For three days, he didn't want to eat and he became weaker and weaker. Someone probably didn't appreciate the fact that there was a guard on duty, and they thought a bit of poison would finish him off. Doris was so attached to him that just seeing him that weak made her weep. He was well liked by all, including most of the Africans, and he would have been greatly missed.

Grass Roofs

Linda and Doris lived in a little grass-roofed house made of stone and mud mortar. The ants crawled up the outside walls, and on the way visited all their relatives who lived in the mortar. Naturally, they arrived on the roof and contributed to the already infested grass. Before the next rainy season in the spring, something needed to be done to the roof, because there were so many rotten spots and maggots dropping continually all over everything. The ladies often had to hold one hand over their food while they ate because of the bugs, grubs, and grass constantly falling from above. They jokingly considered inventing a cup or glass with a lip on it like a mustache cup so that they could drink water without having to pick out the grubs or the grass before taking a swallow.

They decided that instead of constantly cleaning the furniture and floor, they would sweep the inside of the roof and be rid of the grass and visitors once and for all. They removed the furniture and everything from the rooms, and went to work. Ugh. In the process they ended up with dirt, grass, bugs, and larva all over the floor and all over themselves. It didn't solve the problem; they just had to look for more buckets and pans when it rained because of the holes they managed to create in the roof. There was one positive thing about a grass roof, and only one: it made the house much cooler. Sometime later, the roof was changed, and they enjoyed having a much cleaner house and both hands free to feed their tummies.

More Children's Classes

Serving Christ in Africa was not only exciting, but a source of continual blessing when they saw what the Word of God did in the hearts and lives of so many of the children. It took hours of preparation to teach over one hundred children of all ages five mornings a week, but it was exciting to see how God blessed the work. Nearly every day one or more children would accept Christ as their Savior.

On one Sunday, ninety of the children sang "He Arose" in the Sango language in two-part harmony for the morning worship service. Naturally, it wasn't done professionally. How could it be with Doris as their music teacher? However, it was done with joyful hearts as unto the Lord, God was honored, and hearts were touched. On another Sunday, twenty of the children who had memorized I Corinthians 13 recited it together in church. Doris was so excited to see them memorize and recite Scripture. Three of them memorized and recited seventy-two verses in order to receive a New Testament in the Sango language. Can you imagine kids in the United States getting excited about receiving a New Testament?

God's Message

At that time the missionaries hadn't translated the entire Bible into the Sango language, but as the language committee would complete a book of the Bible, Doris would make copies for the children to use as they learned to read. Way back before the Central African Republic gained their independence, the missionaries could see the handwriting on the wall, and felt the urgency of getting God's Word into the hearts and hands of the people. Even the threats of communism around the world helped the missionaries to realize that the more the Africans memorized Scripture, the better equipped they would be to meet the unknown future.

For weeks, to add to the already full program, Doris worked on compiling and writing seventy-two lessons in the Sango language that could be used in Baptist Mid-Missions' children's classes all over the Central African Republic and the Chad Republic. It took literally hundreds of hours to complete the rough draft, all of which had to be worked into the already very heavy daily program. The day that she finished the first draft and sent it off to the language committee, Lorene entered the hospital. That series was eventually completed when other events quieted down a bit.

She did other series, but the one on the book of Exodus was a real winner with the kids. As soon as the book of Exodus was translated into Sango, Doris decided to help the children in the Central African Republic and Chad learn more about the Old Testament by writing lessons on that portion of Scripture. The enthusiasm of the children made it worth all the work, effort, and prayer that went into it. She constantly called on her prayer warriors at home to be her helpers. Many times the program was so heavy that she needed a special unction of strength through the prayers of God's people.

As they did the studies daily, with Exodus as the textbook, the children memorized many scriptures, chapter titles, and the main themes of each chapter. When they had completed the study of that book, those children could have competed and passed an exam of its contents and blessings as well as any Bible school student or pastor. Later, Doris taught classes in the mission's Bible school, and one of the classes was the book of Exodus. Some of the lessons the students learned from the Israelites' journey were a big help to them in the years that followed when the African Christians would suffer much.

The missionaries would get quite tired, but the blessings and joys made it worth the weary bones and concerned tears. In one month alone, there were twelve boys and girls that accepted Jesus as their Savior. It was times like that when the missionaries were reminded that they were ambassadors for Christ. Their joy was to make disciples who could go out and share God's Word and the message of salvation to a dying world. The scriptures tell us that our Savior wept and became weary during His time on earth, and that they were but servants of the King of Kings. He daily renews the strength of those who live for Him and serve Him.

Times of Heartaches, too

Not all of the events and practices rejoiced their hearts. Two of the young girls who Doris had so enjoyed watching grow in the Lord, and had seemed willing to serve Him, left for the initiation rites. Doris was very upset and saddened. These rites, which were the major step from puberty to adulthood, were not just an African custom. Among other things, they involved Satan worship, and all of the initiates were mutilated in one way or another in the circumcision rites, the girls as well as the boys. Doris assisted in delivering babies of more than a few maternity cases in which the poor girl had so much scar tissue that the baby could not be delivered. What needless suffering for young teenagers.

Transfer to Kembe

Due to lack of workers to hold the fort at Kembe, at the field conference, Doris was asked to help out there for a time. The mission station at Kembe is situated between Bambari and Bangassou, the two stations where Doris had previously worked. One Friday morning, awhile later when Doris was stationed there, an urgent call came for Edie Wotherspoon, her co-worker and the nurse on the station to, "Come and help, come and help." Wherever Doris was stationed, if the call for the nurses came during the night, she would accompany them and do what she could to be of help. Sometimes it was no more than to hold the flashlight or kerosene lantern. Many times she even held the patient: the babies she held in her arms and the adults by a neck hold, or something similar, to command cooperation.

That time, the husband of a young girl ready to have a baby wanted to go to the village some distance away to help his wife, but they had no vehicle. Edie told him that he must bring his wife in to the dispensary at the mission station. Lacking the gift of "hurry," he didn't get back to the dispensary with the very young wife of fourteen or fifteen years of age until Saturday morning. Edie worked with her off and on all day, and Doris would jog down to check on things and to see if she could be of help. Just before supper they could find only a very weak pulse. They continued to work with her all evening and into the night by the light of a kerosene lantern. Edie decided that the only thing to do was to try the forceps. Besides the patient being so young and tiny, she had so much scar tissue from the initiation rites that there was very little room for the baby to make its appearance. To add to the problem, she was already so infected from syphilis that Edie and Doris had a real monstrosity of a mess on their hands. Edie was able to insert the forceps, but although they both tried they couldn't get the forceps in position to be able to help the baby be born. They both wore rubber gloves (plastic wasn't available yet), but were getting a bath in the disinfectant during the long hours trying to help this dear girl give birth to her baby. It was only the Lord that gave the strength and the wisdom to do that, but the struggle wasn't over yet. Edie pulled, table and all, as Doris tried to hold the young girl with her feet propped against the table legs. Every minute was a struggle, but after a half hour of using their muscles and God-given wisdom, Edie was able to extract the dead baby. They were fearful that they might lose the mother, too. She hemorrhaged a great deal, combined with all of the infection from the syphilis; they knew that only a miracle from God would keep her alive. Edie worked furiously with antibiotics and TLC. Their patient looked much better when Edie and Doris finally headed for the house, a hot shower, some food, and rest.

Many times this same story repeated itself. Details varied from one case to another, but the missionaries were always reminded that their call was from God to minister first to the souls of sin-darkened people, and then also to the many physical needs that they encountered. The happy ending to this story is that this young girl did hear, and accepted the gospel message that Jesus died for her sins.

Before the husband had brought her in, as was often the custom, the "Old Ones" in the village had treated her. The "Old Ones" reported that even sitting on her and bouncing on her stomach didn't make the baby come out. This was a common practice to help the baby to hurry up and get out of the womb. Then too, this was one of those many cases where the girl had been cut in the initiation rites a couple of years before, which caused scar tissue that didn't stretch for the baby to be born. They had waited so long before bringing this poor girl to the mission station, and had used such severe, harsh methods on her, that it was only thanks to God that her life was spared.

Teenagers

Doris thoroughly enjoyed all of her classes, but she found exceptional delight in her teenage girl's class. Probably some of the heathen practices, such as the initiation rites, had helped to increase her burden for the lives and future of these young girls. They really seemed to enjoy the study of God's Word, and were excited about memorizing long passages of Scripture too. So many things were changing with independence coming to many of the African nations. Hiding God's Word in their hearts was the main goal in all of their classes. The handwriting on the wall indicated that the tremendous welcome that missionaries had always had in that country was becoming less and less evident; they all wondered how much more time they had to love and teach those dear people.

The girls learned to sew by making patchwork skirts from scraps of leftover cloth that Doris had from sewing shirts and dresses for the missionaries in previous years. The excitement ran high as they learned to thread their needles and make stitches in a straight line (that often had to be taken out so that they could try again). Their choices of joining colors and patterns of the cloth squares were very original, but who cared? Many times Doris chuckled to herself all the way home after the sewing bees.

The Saturday before Christmas they had a party for the teenagers who had been faithful in class attendance. They were of an age that they were most needed in the gardens and for other work in their homes. They were very artful in getting as much done at home as possible so that they wouldn't have to miss classes as well as their awards for faithful attendance. Edie and Doris set the table for about thirty curious kids, as very few of them had ever sat at a table to eat before. Edie and Doris wore white blouses and big red bows at the neck, and the African pastor who helped them serve, along with two other fellows, wore white hospital gowns with big red bow ties. Their guests were quite thrilled with the whole affair. The menu was Spanish rice, bananas with peanuts, bread, Kool-Aid, and cake. The dessert dishes were made of used Christmas cards, folded up on the sides and fastened with a staple to keep their shape. The teens were accustomed to eating with their fingers, so they were a bit puzzled with the fork and spoon each found at their place setting. Their solution was to use both at the same time. Playing games and lots of singing together finished off the afternoon.

Kembe, continued

As the girls were often without a vehicle and none of them went hunting, they rarely had meat to eat. The Kembe Falls were not far away, and often the Africans would bring them huge tilapia fish to buy. One fish would feed about twenty people. One day a couple of Arabs came by leading a yearling cow, hoping that the missionaries would want to buy it. Doris did most of the cooking, as the other two girls didn't like to cook, so they voted to let her do the bargaining. "It's practically a gift, but we will let you have it for $16," they said. The missionaries had learned that certain Africans had no notion that they would pay the first price. "I'll give you $10," she said. After dickering a bit, they agreed to the final price of $12. As they had interrupted her dinner Doris went back to eating before it got cold, and although she had made a bargain she didn't run right back out with the money. After a few minutes they sent the cook in to tell her that they would take $10 for the cow. Even though they had assured the girls that it was theirs to sell, it is very possible that they had stolen the cow and couldn't take it back to the village. The Arabs knew that this was their one and only market in that area, since the girls were the only white people around. Lest anyone think that they really got a bargain, they could count every rib on the beast.

Doris told the Africans that maybe they should fatten up the cow before they killed her to eat. They immediately all laughed at her and asked where she thought that she would get food. When she told them that they could feed it grass, they hooted and hollered, "Cows don't eat grass." Even though her Dad wasn't a farmer, they had had a cow and had lived in the country where she had seen hundreds of cows eat grass. The girls tried to tell them that cows in their own country even ate dry grass that is put into barns so that the animals can eat in the wintertime as well. The subject was dropped when they said that these cows were different. However, Molly Mo did eat grass until they butchered her, so she must have changed nationality. The African servant said he knew how to chop it up and chop it up he did! Half of the meat went to the folks in the village and no one seemed to mind that it was chopped. At least they got seasoning for their soup. The girls weren't completely ignorant as they knew where the filet mignon was located, and claimed that before he got to it.

One of the times Doris got quite shook up while she was stationed at Kembe was when several Arabs came to her back door with a small child that had been severely burned. The child was screaming from pain, and then from fright. As soon as they deposited the child in front of the girls, they all left and went out in the field to face Mecca to say their prayers, leaving the screaming, hurting child to the care of the girls. They had received no explanation of how the child had gotten in that condition, and Edith and Doris were in a quandary as to how they could help the child. They tried to get the attention of someone in the group who had brought the child to them to be doctored, but they had their faces and bodies bowed down to the ground in their religious practice. Was devotion the name of the game, or was lack of love or compassion ruling their actions? This was one occasion where, had the motto, "What would Jesus do?" been practiced, the picture would have been quite different. With grateful hearts that someone had cared about them and had told them the gospel, Edith and Doris proceeded to look to Him for wisdom, and cared for the child with compassion. Doris was reminded once again that they had been called, "To open their eyes, and to turn them from darkness to light, and from the power of Satan unto God, that they may receive forgiveness of sins, and inheritance among them which are sanctified by faith that is in Me" (Acts 26:18). Only eternity will tell the results of compassionate and caring hearts that have ministered to millions throughout the ages and around the world in His name.

Doris enjoyed the ministry that God gave her during her time at Kembe. God blessed His Word always, and in so many ways. In just a couple of months, over forty children realized that they were sinners, and openly confessed their need of Christ as their Savior. Doris headed out for children's chapel at 7:30 each morning, and returned to the house a little after noon. She taught two hours in Sango, the trade language, followed by two hours of teaching in French. Her main purpose was to teach the Word of God. This was done through Bible stories, songs about the Lord Jesus, and memorization of passages from the Bible. The last two hours of the morning were more than filled up by reading, writing, and arithmetic in both languages. Her teenage girls' class followed in the afternoons because they were needed in the morning hours to help in the gardens and homes. Many of these girls lived in homes and villages where they were slaves to family and friends. Doris needed much guidance from her dear Heavenly Father to help them know how to live to honor the Lord.

Girls were bought and sold at a very early age. The girls were not thought of very highly in their culture, and thus had many temptations and sinkholes along the way. They were taught that they couldn't decide anything for themselves. As a rule, they had no say in matters, and often thought that it was a natural way of life to submit to one and all before salvation. It was not an easy class for Doris to teach, but the need was so great. Once again, with a compassionate heart given from the Lord, she loved each one and shared with them how much our Heavenly Father loved them and wanted only good things and happiness for them all.

On one occasion, Doris learned that one of the girls was pregnant, and, of course, that saddened her heart. Their temptations were as great as anywhere else because their enemy, Satan, wanted to make a mess of their lives. They were often from unsaved families whose thoughts were mainly on how much dowry they could get for their daughters or sister. Even Christian families were sometimes impatient for the dowry, and neglected to check if the fellow was truly a born-again believer. One sad case happened to one of her dear girls. The fellow assured her family that he was a Christian, and that he had no wives. You guessed it—after all of the exchanges took place, the sad discovery was made that he already had two wives back in the village.

In the afternoons, six days a week, Doris taught high school English and science to one of the missionary kids. Doris was sure that she spent more time preparing than her student did. Kids will be kids regardless of where they are. They had to do some doubling up to meet the Teachout's schedule for furlough. Imagine, if you can, a freshman in high school obliged to take classes on Saturday.

Doris had the desire and the responsibility to write children's lessons in the Sango language. These lessons were to be used in the children's ministries in which that language was spoken and understood, mainly in the Central African Republic and Chad, where there was an urgent need for such lessons. In one prayer letter, she mentioned that she needed forty hours a day since forty hours a week wasn't sufficient to fit the lessons into the daily program. Wisdom was needed to determine how to take care of what was important, and not get side-tracked by what was urgent.

One of their big needs at that time was a vehicle. They lived twelve kilometers from the post, and it was quite a hike to mail a letter or buy food staples. Of course when they bought flour, they had meat, too. That far from civilization, you could be assured that the flour that came from a barrel at the local store would be the living quarters for plenty of weevils. By the time the flour got to the middle of Africa, it was so old that many little wiggly worms and bugs had come along for the ride.

Presently, they were having a conference at the riverside. There must have been over a thousand people attending the "bring your own chair" morning service. While waiting for her turn to teach the pastors and evangelists how to tell Bible stories, Doris had chosen a spot with a cool breeze under a shade tree. However, in very short order, the breeze no longer existed when a circle of about fifty folks had gathered around her. Thinking that they might have questions, Doris asked why so many had gathered there. Their answer, full of blarney, couldn't have been clearer if it had come directly from Ireland: "Don't we all have hunger just to look at your face?" Frankly, probably some of them were having a heyday watching Doris' left hand in action as she was writing a letter. Not many of them knew how to write, but they sure didn't know how to do it with their left hand. They probably thought that it was a special gift. Well, it was, wasn't it?

A Bump in the Road

"No one has been playing ball here in my bedroom," Doris thought to herself as she rolled over on to what she thought was a baseball. After a thorough and fruitless search of her bed, she realized that the bump that she had hit wasn't in the bed but on her body. Now what? There were no doctors closer than a long day's journey, so off they went for a ride in the back of a pick-up. At the mission hospital, Dr. Fisher told Doris she needed to get a flight out to Cleveland, Ohio as soon as possible. There at Ippy she was a long day's journey from her home at Kembe, with no vehicle of her own. How would she be able to get back to Kembe and then on to Bangui, which was a two-day trip from home, to catch a plane? They had no telephone service, so she communicated with the missionaries stationed at Bangui by slow telegram service of her urgent need for a flight out as soon as possible. As all of this was taking place over a period of a couple of weeks, which was a short time considering they were in the interior of a land-locked African country, the Lord reminded Doris of the poem written by E.G Wellesley-Wesley that she had printed on her last prayer card. Full dosage of these truths needed to be inhaled, swallowed and believed:

> "The steps of the way I know not,
> but My Leader know full well:
> My hand is in His,
> I fear not—in the depths of His peace I dwell.
>
> He knows where He leads; I know not,
> but I trust in His love each day:
> My heart is His own;
> I fear not, for the way is my Lord's highway.
>
> The hours may seem dark and dreary,
> but His presence my life shall cheer;
> The dark may seem dark and dreary,
> but I know that my Lord is near.

Jesus Led Me All the Way

One step at a time He shows me,
and I know that the rest He hides,
That love may the better show me
how in safety His mercy guides.

I wait, in His will abiding; I rejoice,
for His strength sustains:
I trust in His Word confiding;
and of doubt not one trace remains.

And never comes pain or sadness
but to hasten the sunlit morn;
The grief shall give way to gladness,
that never a sigh be born."

Although she finally had a flight booked, it wasn't a jet or a very recent model, and a stop in Libya for motor repairs was a necessity. Kaddafi ruled with an iron hand even in the 1960s; no one was to leave the plane during that stop for repairs. They were without electricity, air conditioning, fans, or water, and the interior of the plane was extremely hot in that tropical climate. The Lord gave Doris liberty in talking about the Lord to a Jewish man seated beside her. He was polite and listened for a while and then he said as he showed her his wallet, "This is my god." Her heart cried for him, and for the millions out there that hadn't trusted Christ as the real source of riches.

The plane was finally in the air, and they arrived in Paris. As was the usual pattern, a missionary from that area, either a resident or someone in language study, helped her get to the next plane. After an eight-hour flight to New York City and then another flight to Cleveland, Ohio, she immediately became a patient in the Huron Road Hospital.

The first words the doctor uttered when Doris woke up after the procedure were, "We can praise the Lord that all of this is past and look forward to great things from Him in the future." The days and weeks of anxiety in the process of getting from the interior of Africa to the actual operation were over. Nearly a month of anxiety had passed over many unknown details from the time that Doris discovered the lump until the surgery. She had written a little poem as a prayer just before she left Africa:

"If you had seen their flowing tears
as they bid me a fond goodbye.

If you could hear, 'We're praying,
Miss,' you'd understand just why.

My heart just aches as I leave once more
but our God above,
Will bring me back to them again,
with the message of His love."

Doris had a heavy heart thinking about all the dear ones in Africa to whom she'd like to be ministering. As is usually the case when it is an emergency furlough, she had the indebtedness to take care of before she could return to the field. Her dear Lord was with her all the way and her dear, caring prayer partners fervently prayed.

Back Home Again

Shortly, she was back in Africa, and back into the full swing of things at the station at Kembe. At four in the morning, she rolled out of bed to start the charcoal fire to heat the tub of water for laundry. By five-thirty, after much coaxing, the washing machine gave up being ornery, and Doris was able to start the washing. Now, why did she insist on starting the wash at that hour? Everything had to be washed, rinsed, wrung out, and hung up before she started classes at 7:45.

The cast of about sixty children was going to present a program in church in a couple of days. Doris was probably the one the most excited and nervous because she was, for the first time, helping them to sing in two-part harmony and in two languages, Sango and French. Even though she used her good old faithful accordion to help keep the tune, it didn't come naturally for them to want to speed things up much.

One of her teenage girls was getting married the next Sunday, and her friends were having a hey-day thinking of ways to get her decked out in white for the event. Doris finally had the inspiration to make the veil out of mosquito netting with little bows on it that she made out of ribbon from packages she had received. There was no money paid for the bride in this wedding. The parents, who were born again, didn't want their daughter treated like an animal being sold at the market. Since most girls were still being bought by their husbands-to-be, the missionaries were thrilled to see the love and honor given to their daughter by her parents.

God delighted the hearts of the missionaries repeatedly. One of the African lay leaders who had gone to a neighboring village to preach the gospel, returned to Kembe and continued to preach the message of salvation. A man in the village accepted Christ as his Savior, and before the preacher returned to the mission station, the man said, "I want to give you something that I have in my house." It was a conglomeration of native medicine, which the preacher accepted and brought back with him. In the midst was a piece of charred wood. The new convert told him that the belief was that if it were lighted enough to make a smudge, and the smoke blew on someone that they didn't like, it would kill them. How many, many times missionaries are asked why they sacrifice their lives to live among such depravity and darkness. Only eternity will give the full explanation when they walk the streets of gold with those who were reached with the gospel message of the one true God's love for them.

Where is the Need Greatest?

Although the field conference in November gave her permission to return to Bangassou early in the following year, for the time being the need appeared to be greater at Kembe. Doris returned to Kembe to fill in for the nurse who needed a vacation. Doris had told her that she would only take care of the urgent cases, such as babies with high temperatures from malaria. Remember the station was twelve miles from the post. One mother complained of an extreme pain in her stomach, so Doris felt compelled to break the rule of "babies only." Wow! Did that start things! "You took care of her, so why can't you care for me too?" was the question several times a day. Doris, being a soft touch for them, soon was ministering to all of them about four hours a day, plus the emergencies at night.

She was still enjoying the classes for the kids and teenagers too. On December first, the children from the mission station marched in the Independence Day parade at the post at Kembe. It was a real honor to be invited by the Sous-Prefet, the government official in command at that time, to be a part of the parade. Doris ordered material and the parents paid for the children's outfits. Blue and red were the colors available. The African pastor, with the help of two or three others, made up the outfits while the missionaries were at their annual conference. The children did a great job of keeping in step as they sang Christian songs both in French and in Sango. Can't you just see them proudly carrying the flag of the Republic as well as the Christian flag? (A Betsy Ross Gilbert made the flags). Doris wonders how she managed to find all five of the different colored cloth needed to make them. They also carried a banner with Acts 16:31 printed on it in both languages.

Doris was grateful to the Lord for the blessings He gave her in the ministry at Kembe. God's hand of blessing on His Word was her joy, as there were as many as forty children saved in the last two months before she left to go back to Bangassou. She was glad to be there to meet physical needs from time to time, but preparing so many for eternity by sharing the message of salvation several times a day was worth all the physical fatigue and heartfelt sorrows. The following little song came to mind: "I've had many tears and sorrows; I've had questions for tomorrow, there've been times I didn't know right from wrong, but in every situation, God gave blessed consolation that my trials only came to make me strong."

Doris needed to go back to Bambari to pick up the things she had left there when she went to Kembe to help out temporarily for two years. The barrels she had sent out at the time of her furlough two years previously finally arrived and were at Bambari as well. Some repacking and adjusting needed to be done with the barrels. There was surely expired boxed food, and other things that would be classed as garbage that needed to be sorted out. Then too, there were things in the barrels for other missionaries, the workers at the work at Bambari, and for other nearby stations.

Back East at Bangassou

Doris received a letter from one of the teenage boys who had been in her classes concerning her departure from Kembe: "Miss, this thing that you have done to us is not nice. How could you just walk off and leave us? Please write to tell us that we can come to you there."

When Doris arrived back at Bangassou, the need for a new house was reemphasized. The grass roof had become much worse, and the termites had eaten up the door frames and window sills. It looked as if the need was very urgent. Not only was there a need for funds to do it, but also for someone to help get it done. Everyone's schedule was already so full. They didn't know how to figure out the whole equation, but they knew that God cared more about it than they did, and would take care of it in His own timing.

One Friday they had a literal "hay" day. With barrels on top of tables and brooms fastened to long sticks, they proceeded to sweep the grass roof from the inside. It reminded the girls of throwing down hay for the cows back on the farm. Probably the cows back home wouldn't even have attempted to eat the grass that they swept down. When the wind blew, there was still a lot of litter falling on their heads and with rainy season there was lots of rain coming down on their heads as well. They ran out of pans and buckets, so they just let the water drip all over the place. The floor was mud bricks, as Doris found out shortly after arriving in Africa; mud bricks plus rainy roof equals a mess. Doris kept a big piece of plastic over her mosquito net and bed to protect from the armies of mosquitoes and gnats during rainy season. The jungle grew right up to the back step of their house. The Lord wonderfully preserved their health in spite of all these little visitors. Doris did look like a teenager with acne from all of the kisses contributed by the little varmints that came to visit.

High winds and rains were doing a number on the buildings on the mission station at Bangassou, as well as on the African's houses in the village. It was probably a hurricane, but they weren't labeled that back then. Shortly before Christmas, trees and houses crashed to the ground, and the roof from the dispensary was lifted off entirely and set down in another field with hardly a dent in the aluminum. The missionaries all made a mad dash to try and save the medical equipment and the medications. Bandages and medicines were strewn all over, and they tried hard to recover as much as possible. Needless to say, it took more effort getting things back in place than it had taken for them to be dispersed.

At Bangassou, there was a very good interest in classes for all, children and adults. About five hundred children and teenagers attended Sunday school classes and junior church, and around two thousand adults gathered for church services each week. Their prayer was that growth in spiritual things would keep pace with the attendance. They never ran out of space; they just squeezed in more on the benches. The seating was made for twelve hundred, and they managed to increase the seating to twenty-five hundred, but there was still the overflow crowd on the outside. The method was simple: go to the middle of the bench full of people, turn around, and start wiggling yourself into a space that those seated didn't realize existed.

On Saturdays, the missionaries took the teachers in groups to train them to teach the Sunday school lessons. Some of the teachers did an excellent job of sharing the truths of God's Word, but many of them had very little or no schooling, and were not fluent readers. Teaching people to read was one of the classes on the schedule for all ages, but it took them a good bit of time to both read the words and understand what they read.

Although Doris didn't know how to ride a bike, she purchased one and determined that it would be a big help in getting from one class to another in the short allotted time, supposedly with less energy expended. She wasn't getting any younger, and her determined personality convinced her that she could conquer a little thing like that. On one occasion, she fell and the pedal engraved a nice big gash on her left leg. When asked if she would be getting back on it she said, "The bike won't do me much good just setting on the veranda, will it?" She hopped back on and wobbled back home.

A Road Trip to Ouango

This was the conversation between Ruth and Doris as they planned a trip to Ouango: "Are you taking your raincoat?"

"It's awfully dirty and needs to be washed before I wear it again."

"What if it rains? Remember, there is no window in the door on the driver's side of the truck."

"It doesn't look like rain. I'll put a quilt in to hang on the door in case it does rain. Perhaps I should ask Dean if he thinks that it is safe to drive to Ouango with that leaf missing in the left front spring."

Later, "What did Dean say?"

"He said that he thought that it would be safe. He also put it on the pit, checked underneath, and said the oil, water, battery and brake fluid were good to go. I am glad that I asked him about that spring, aren't you?"

"Do you think that we should go to Ouango with a broken windshield?"

"Oh yes, we can wear sun glasses so that we don't get bugs in our eyes. Then too, there is a little bit of windshield left on the driver's side that will help to give me some vision."

"Maybe I could make a windshield with screen wire and saran wrap."

"Mmm… do you think that would hold?"

"Nothing ventured, nothing had."

"All ready; let's go."

Ruth and Doris left from Bangassou to go to Ouango at 1:30 p.m. on a Saturday afternoon. Ouango was one of the mission stations about sixty kilometers from Bangassou. The Nimmo's, who were normally stationed at Ouango, had loaned their truck to the girls when they went home on furlough. The girls decided to take a quick trip over to encourage the dear ones there in the work of the Lord and to check out things at the Nimmo's house.

Their trip was an adventure, filled with excitement all the way. By the time they had left the village and arrived at the main road, the saran wrap had popped several times. They more or less expected that, and both had worn scarves because of the wind. What they weren't expecting was the downpour of heavy rain that started when they were about halfway to their destination. With no window on the driver's side and no windshield, they were not only sitting in water, they were drinking it. Ruth used a washcloth and a hanky alternately to wipe the little piece of windshield so that Doris could see to drive. The rain came down in sheets, making it difficult to see very far ahead, and in many places the entire road was a stream of water. Three or four times they were forced to come to a complete stop due to zero visibility. The Lord traveled right along with them, and they were thankful they had made the effort to come when they saw how glad the dear Christians were to see them. They were pleased that someone cared enough to come even during a storm to worship with them. The girls enjoyed the time and the fellowship with the folks there. As usual, some of them had many questions and problems to share. They shared, cried, and prayed with the missionaries, with much heart searching and the reading of God's Word.

At least one leader from that area was a very proud man and sought to have the dear brothers and saints bow down to him. They were accustomed to having a chief in their villages, and this man tried to take the position of a chief in the churches in that area. Some seemed to think that it was a natural process, although it caused much fear and unrest. If he said that they must work in his garden or coffee plantation before they could be baptized, they were convinced that this was part of being a Christian and humbly obeyed. But other dear brothers and sisters were frustrated and saddened as they saw things happening contrary to the message in God's Word. In contrast, the Nimmos, the resident missionaries home on furlough, loved the people dearly. They were sweet, dear, humble servants who also loved and obeyed God's Word. The sincere Christians, who had such thankful hearts that someone had cared enough to come to them with the gospel, recognized that the other leader's unchristian attitude was not God honoring. Needless to say, Satan was happy with the unrest and the uplifting of man rather than God.

As the girls returned with heavy hearts to Bangassou, they weren't thinking about the little inconvenience of a broken windshield, broken spring, or windowless car door as much as they thought of and prayed for God's little ones they had left behind. Both were asking the Lord to help them verbalize in prayer letters to folks back home the need to pray hard for the brothers and sisters in Africa:

"Do you care for souls, my brother?
Care enough to spend an hour
On your knees in fervent prayer?

Tears and prayer break Satan's power,
Pray the Lord of all the harvest
He will send His workers;

Pray for the children, for the sinners,
Christian pray, and pray, and pray."

The Light Plant Took a Vacation

Well, they were back to using the circulation heater because their old, remodeled, fixed up light plant wasn't working again. They were keeping company with the Aladdin lamps again. The bugs were circulating and the lamps gave off extra heat—very cozy--ugh!

The pace of programs was very tiring. One day, as soon as breakfast was over, she went to the church to set up the benches in a little room in back of the church where she would have children's class later on. After lugging the benches around, Doris had a music class for the wives of Bible school students. That class finished at 9 a.m. and she rushed back to the church to have classes with the children until 11 a.m. Fixing and eating lunch came next, and after preparing for the sewing class, she dashed off to teach hygiene class. Sewing class followed and continued until 5 p.m. While heating the soup for their supper, she decided to start a prayer letter on her good old faithful typewriter. Whoops—cough, cough, clap, clap. Just then Zacharius came for his milk. She had gone to the Department of Agriculture to ask about getting surplus milk for the children there. They had been encouraged to believe that it might be a reality in the near future.

Back to the Typewriter

"We haven't heard from you recently," was the message from home. How else could she have been able to write all these details in a book if she hadn't been faithful in sending prayer letters? Praise the Lord for dear ones who saved her letters. The girls repeatedly reminded people to pray for their roof because naturally, it wasn't in the nature of grass roofs to have a tendency to improve. In the midst of this inconvenience, the Lord reminded Doris that He had no place to lay His head. Reminders like that were necessary and contributed to a happy heart.

A little four-year-old girl would come to children's class with continuously runny sores all over her legs. Her little dress that was clean when she came was soon a sticky mess. She would scratch the oozing sores until her fingers were covered with blood and runny matter. During the service, Doris went to the house to get some bandages and covered the sores on her legs. She told the little dear that she would need to go to the dispensary the next day. It wasn't always the case, but the mother did bring her, and with ten days of treatment the sores were nearly gone.

On her way to teach in the Bible school a few days later, Doris saw the mother and child. She proceeded to ask the lady if she was saved. "No, I'm not," was the answer she gave. Doris then asked her if she knew where she would go when she died. Once again the answer was negative. Doris proceeded to tell her about Jesus and that He came to die for sinners. When she told her that all she had to do was confess her sins to Jesus and ask Him to save her soul, the lady answered, "But I can't; I am a baptized Catholic." Doris continued witnessing to her, and before she went on to class, the mother prayed and asked Jesus to be her Savior. With joy and rejoicing both went on their way thanking God for His love. This made one more born-again child of God for whom to pray. Doris had simply shared the precious message that Jesus died to save sinners.

When the news came through that President Kennedy had been shot, it was a shock not only to the missionaries, the only Americans in the area, but also to the officials at the post. Both African and French officials came out to offer their condolences to all of the American citizens. The radio from Bangui played requiem music for two or three days. Even though it was in honor of a sad occasion, it was a welcome improvement over the "rock and ruin" noise that was the usual menu.

Lessons and Living

Doris was on the committee to write programs and class material in the Sango language for use in the Central African Republic and Chad Republic. To meet with the committee at Bangui, five hundred miles away, took lots of planning. Communication with the others on the committee was almost non-existent. They could go into the post and send a ten-word telegram, if the message was urgent. The mail truck came once a week when the roads were passable. The missionaries knew that there was always a solution if things were done for God's glory. When the roads were passable Doris could make the two-day trip to Bangui. Or there might be a propeller plane coming in soon, but, even if it did, would it be coming back in the near future? How could she afford time away from her classes for the students, children, and others that already filled her days? She knew that God cared more than she did, and that He had promised the strength to do "all things" that He had planned for her, but it took a lot of committing on her part. She waited on the Lord to show her how He wanted her to use her time and strength, and most of all her entire life. Separating the *important* from the *urgent* was not easy for her even on a daily basis, let alone planning the weeks ahead with so many unknowns and so much to do.

Classes for the Bible school were about to get underway again. The men had planned the classes with God's direction, and the hours of the day were going to be extra full of teaching for all of the missionaries and helpers. Four classes were in session simultaneously, starting early each morning: one in the Bible school building, one in the children's chapel, and two in the church. Those classes, combined with the afternoon classes in the carpenter's shop kept the station humming all day long.

Doris alone would be teaching two hours a day in the Bible school: Old and New Testament, Proverbs, Ecclesiastes, and Song of Solomon. "Any notes you can share?" was her request for help from pastors in the United States. She taught the children two hours a day and the teen-age girls three hours daily, a women's class three hours weekly, Sunday school teachers for one hour weekly, and French school children for one hour on Saturday. Then there was Sunday school and Junior Church to supervise. Lessons had to be translated into the Sango language, written up, and printed for outstation work as well as sent to the other works in the country. "Help" was her heart cry as it went out to her prayer partners and faithful supporters. She was already training teachers and helpers to help carry the load. God reminded her that His plan and program for her was perfect and if she was trying to do too much, it wasn't His plan.

Not many people realize what a big helper a gasoline motor washing machine can be. One of the missionaries who would not be returning to the field had a nice, nearly new washing machine for sale for $50. The special gifts Doris received for Christmas paid for the washing machine. Had they bought a new one it would have cost $300, and they didn't have $300 above their budget that they could spend. They prayed that they would have wisdom in the care of it so that it would last a long time. Washing that previously required two days to do on the scrub board could now be done in two hours. It was rightfully named, "missionary in training." The machine did require special coaxing at times, but the girls already knew how to clean the spark plug and other little tricks to keep the motor running.

Another step was taken in getting a new house built. A missionary had brought out some nice windows and doors with screens (what luxury), plus some electrical wiring to be used in the house that she was going to build. Because she was now stationed where there was sufficient lodging already, she didn't need these things anymore. Knowing how great the need was for them to build a house, and convinced that the Lord was leading, Doris took on the indebtedness of $1100 to purchase these materials. It was a government requirement that the mission construct permanent dwellings, otherwise the girls would have been content to build another grass-roofed home. Although the guards came out from the government post on a regular schedule to see how the permanent building was progressing, the missionaries had the conviction that building lives for Christ must keep first place in their hearts and schedules.

Ruth and Doris were saddened when their sweet little white fluffy kitten died, but they soon found out that the story didn't end there. It was discovered that it had likely died of rabies. Since three sweet little girls had really enjoyed playing with the kitten, shots for rabies were in order. Poor four-year-old Cathy Chasteen, four-year-old Suzanne Townes, two-year-old Sara Townes, and Doris (old enough to know better) needed to have fifteen shots each of anti-rabies serum right in their tummies. Doris gave the injections (yep, in her own tummy as well) and the girls were promised some candy if they didn't cry. It was very hard for Sara, the two-year-old, to keep the tears back, but she tried really hard.

As a result of the rabies scare, our other mousetraps (cats) had to be shot. One mother cat was about to give birth, and the girls had planned on doing a Caesarean section. They dashed around getting rubber gloves, a knife, and a razor blade. However, the men on the station advised against doing the procedure. Phooey, they all lost out on that exciting experience.

Christmas Again, December, 1968

The canopy of mango trees in front of the girl's home provided a natural theater for the five thousand people who gathered to come see the Christmas program, with their veranda as the stage. Many arrived carrying their little cane stools on their on their heads, giving them the advantage of wiggling into the best spaces if they could find them, while the others would be obliged to sit on the ground.

The children did a great job with the Christmas play entitled, "Why did Jesus Come?" The first scene was of the Garden of Eden showing how sin came into the world and the need of a Savior to redeem us from sin. It was for this that Jesus came into the world as a lowly babe, thus the Christmas story. The Easter story was of Christ when He offered Himself as a sacrifice for sin, that we might be saved if we asked for forgiveness for our own personal sins. Dean Chasteen wrapped it all up with a salvation message telling of God's love for each one present. The idea of love was not a subject about which the most of them had any knowledge. Most of the women had no idea that they had the right to make a personal decision about anything. As strange as it may seem, this was true for many of the men as well, since they were under village rule. By God's grace, the missionaries had the joy of seeing so much change in the lives of their African brothers and sisters to whom they were sent when they accepted the gospel message of Jesus' love for each one of them.

The Africans were slaves, both men and women, long before any of them were sold and brought to America. The verses in Acts 26:18 that Doris had on one of her prayer cards told why they were there in that country: "To open their eyes and to turn them from darkness to light, and from the power of Satan unto God, that they may receive forgiveness of sins, and inheritance among them which are sanctified by faith that is in me."

Even Nurses Get Sick

Doris' co-worker and the nurse at the Bangassou station, Ruth Nephew, had not been well. Her trip to Bangui to diagnose the problem was not successful. The extreme pain in her chest was due to pleurisy, which had been dragging her down for two to three months. The girls decided that a trip to the mission hospital was the next step to take. They left Bangassou at 4 a.m. and arrived at Ippy about 5:30 p.m. the same day. The next day, after the medical check up by the doctor, they started on their way back to Bangassou on the back road by way of Bakouma. Well, at least that was their plan. At the Hyrra Banda ferry they were told that the ferry was broken down and it would be at least four days before it would be useable. "Where to now?" they wondered. Rather than return to Ippy, they took a short cut by way of Kembe. This secondary road should have been called "thirty-secondary road." To help make the trip more eventful, they got on the wrong road in one place and a bridge broke as they crossed it. Then they came to a dead end. In horror, they realized that they'd have to cross back over the same bridge that had broken with them when they crossed it. On the first trip across the logs had skidded away, which meant no way of crossing the second time. It wasn't with hearts filled with glee as they anticipated what was ahead. They asked the Lord to give them wisdom and strength for the task. With lots of huffing and puffing and about two hours in the rain, they rolled those logs in place, thus rebuilding a bridge.

Can you imagine the heft of those logs that were designed to hold up a car? When the logs were in line with the wheels of the truck, Ruth guided while Doris drove across the logs. It might sound as if they went calmly through that display with brave energy. Not so. Both were trembling during the whole procedure, but the operation was successful. A prayer meeting of thanksgiving to God, joyfully praising Him, was their next matter of business. That short cut of about 125 miles took ten hours. Go ahead and laugh. They did. The most important part of the trip was God's protection and direction to get back to the main highway. It was dirt road of course, but much better, and they only had to cut two trees out of the road on this national highway. Well, they did have a flat tire before they got back home. That was a minor issue, as they had both had lots of practice of changing tires. "Just one more thing—" as Colombo would say—the transmission acted up a bit and Doris was unable to shift into reverse or low.

Another surprise was in store for them as they drove into the mission station at Bangassou. The folks back at the station were not spared from exciting activities. On Saturday night, a tornado had ripped through the area and lifted the roof completely off of the storeroom in back of the girl's house. Both of their offices were in that building, and of course things were in quite a mess. Ruth's office had the most damage. It could have been a lot worse, as no one was injured in the storm, although the storm did a major job of rearranging many things at their home and on the entire station. The aluminum roof, which had been lifted off by the storm, was hardly damaged; the puzzle was how to lift it back in place.

Back to Business as Usual

As mentioned before, Doris was chosen of the Lord to help the women in the Eastern part of our field to organize a *Be ta ouali* or "Faithful Women's" group in each of the organized churches. The whole idea was very foreign to women who had only known a life of slavery and labor. Repeatedly, they were considered by the male population as their servants, and useful only for producing sons and daughters. The purpose of the group was to help the women help other women and to bring them to a knowledge of Christ. It was a very delicate situation, but the African pastors as a rule were enthusiastic about a special program for their wives and other ladies of their churches. Even the government was enthused about the special program.

In one week, Doris added four meetings with the women in the area churches. She went to the Ouango area over the weekend to encourage the ladies there. A couple of pastors weren't enthusiastic about the women being considered as true human beings, which caused some major problems later. Truly, this was a program designed to help, encourage, enthuse, and educate the dear ladies to have a heart's desire to know and serve our Lord. Doris cried, "I can't do this," but in her walk with the Lord, He reminded her that she wasn't there in that country to show her strength and importance. The Lord had called and enabled her to be there to uplift the name of Christ and to serve Him. Their classes and other ministries continued to be a blessing to their hearts even if at times their bodies got a bit weary. The release time classes in the government schools were encouraged by the government, which was a real blessing and an encouragement to the missionaries and their helpers. The house-to-house ministry done by the Faithful Women's groups continued to be blessed by our dear Lord, and there were 129 professions of faith in one month. All this helped them rejoice in spite of the bumps in the road called troubles and pains. To quote F.B. Meyer, "Every event that comes to you will link you by a golden clasp to the love of God."

Early in March, representatives, pastors, and missionaries from all self-supporting Baptist churches in the Central African Republic met together. The thought was that unity would bring more strength. The fellowship and sharing served to endear and encourage one another. It is not just a matter of different nationalities and colors working together, but also many tribes and languages. Dean Chasteen, one of the missionaries from our station, was one of the concerned ones that met with the group numerous times to help them in planning and preparing the association for the entire field.

God repeatedly reminded Doris as she called for wisdom and direction that He was God. Hebrews, chapter eleven was one of the passages of Scripture that was a real dose of encouragement as she continued to count on Him for His help, direction, and blessing. These dear ladies needed to know that God loved them, and that we loved them, and we wanted them to know the delight of loving and serving God. "Beloved, now are we the sons of God." Doris often cried to God in prayer for a greater love for Him and for the dear ones to whom she was to minister: "The love of God constrains us," and I John 5:2: "By this we know that we love the children of God, when we love God."

Did you ever note that a bride in love is a woman in bloom; her eyes grow bright and her skin grows clear, her beauty blossoms like a flower because her beloved holds her dear? It is even more so if you realize that we who are saved are God's sons, loved with the depths of love He gives through the begotten Son of His? We are loved of God through eternity. Can you understand how we who are sons of God and joint heirs with Christ can be blinded to the poor, despondent or sad; our eyes don't see the dying world around us.

Crisis in the Congo, Just Across the River

In a concerned letter home, Doris wrote of one of many reports for the urgent need of prayer for their neighbors across the river in the Belgian Congo. They had gotten their independence from Belgium just a few weeks previously. She wrote, "His arm is not shortened" (comforting words referring to their Almighty God), in view of the many tragedies that had happened and continued to happen just across the Mbomou River in back of their house. Many of the Norwegian missionaries from Belgian Congo had already sought refuge at their mission station in Bangassou, Central African Republic. "The Congo seems hopeless," was the remark of one of the Norwegian missionaries who was presently with them. She was one of four missionaries who had spent three weeks in Stanleyville during the awful time when the rebels were taking over. Two drunken rebel soldiers had escorted them from Stanleyville to Bouta. The rebels kept shooting their guns out of the window of the vehicle, requiring one of the ladies to hand them bullets as they were needed.

When they returned to their station at Monga, they were "invited" to attend an execution at the post the next day. To be invited means that you do what they say or else it will be your turn next. They crossed the hippo-infested river to the Bangassou station during the night on Sunday. At the time, there were three families and three single ladies with them. Two families and two other singles were still in the troubled areas across the river. The Congolese had crossed over by the hundreds, not only at Bangassou, but at Ouango, as well. The one missionary who was normally stationed over there nearest them went back over to get some things. In a matter of minutes after she arrived back across to the Bangassou side, the rebels were at the bank of the river. They had taken the man who was building the girls' new house. They went over the same evening and saw that her house was still standing. The police from their side of the river said that as they watched with binoculars, load after load of the missionary's possessions were taken from the house. The gunshots, accompanied by hideous screams and songs, could be heard from their side of the river at Bangassou.

Thora, a Norwegian missionary, and Gene Townes were down at the river trying to get cement over by canoe for the girls' house, which was slowly being built as the time and materials were available. They were able to get twelve of the fifteen sacks across the river before the rebels got there. Understandably, most of the Africans ran when they heard the rebels in the area. They had heard that some heathen God had blessed the rebels. Supposedly, the rebels could not be killed. The rebels had just two guards and a chauffeur to overpower the missionaries. Because of all the superstitions, the people were afraid to attack the rebels because they had heard that the car had been baptized in the name of this heathen God. The story was the same for all of the houses the rebels had burned down, and hundreds of Africans present were afraid to stop them. The rebels held mock trials and killed many people right at the post. The missionaries didn't think that they were in danger over on their side of the river. Needless to say, they were saddened by what had and continued to happen to many of their brothers and sisters in Christ. The Lord increased their ministry of hospitality to these needy people without a home.

Two Months Later

From a prayer letter, 1964: "Events continued to escalate in the Belgian Congo. They still knew very little about Dr. Paul Carlson, missionary with the Swedish Covenant Mission in the Congo, other than that he may be a prisoner in Stanleyville. The rebels controlled Monga, about forty-five miles from the mission here in Bangassou. There have been several executions there recently. About one week later, the rebels went to the house of Yansere, one of the deacons of the Monga church and father of eight children. They told him to dress in his best clothes, eat a big dinner, and then come to the post to be executed. When he asked them why they couldn't kill him right there in his home, they told him that he was such a prosperous and well known person, and so much like the white man that he deserved the honor of a public execution. Upon arrival at the place where he was to be executed, they tied him and placed him before the people. They then asked if there were any there who didn't want the deacon killed. The pastor and several others stepped forward. The pastor was asked to pray first, and then the deacon. Once more, the question was repeated to the crowd. Due to fear for their own lives, the cry came up from the remaining people, "Kill him, kill him." A man who lived just across the river from their station fired the gun and hit Yansere in the forehead. He fell to the ground, but didn't die until they put another bullet into his heart. After this execution, many of the people fled into the woods for fear of their lives. Some of the missionaries had met and highly respected Yansere. God's Word promises us that we'll see him again in heaven."

We learned that two more missionaries had been killed at Stanleyville, one of which was Dr. Carlson. This event was much in the international news. His wife had stayed with them at Bangassou a few days before going on the States. The rebels were killing off all the national and international leaders that were there. Even school teachers who had a bit of education were murdered, all of which caused a real setback to any programs of progress in the Congo. Before their independence, the Congo had better roads, better commercial opportunities, and was much advanced over the CAR and Chad, both situated further inland from the coast. The people were led to believe that they would automatically be richer if they got rid of the leaders.

Six months later, there was still more bloodshed, bringing more sorrow and oppression in the Congo. Reports were still coming in of those suffering from hunger and others continued to be massacred.

Their hearts were heavy with the burden for those dear ones over there. Much heartache was caused for both the missionaries and the Africans.

What Was Coming to the CAR?

There was no way that they could fully explain the tension that grew in the CAR during this time, in this country that was getting its independence just a couple of months following that of the neighboring countries. The missionaries remained in constant readiness to leave, with special papers and suitcases packed with emergency necessities. They prepared and had worked up codes for secret communications within the mission, as well as to special contacts in the United States. Bangassou was one of the furthermost points of evacuation. Hurrying to leave wasn't uppermost on the minds of these dear ones who were there in the country because of God's calling. Their call went out for prayer that the doors to the gospel ministry would remain open to these dear people. It was a natural reaction, at times, for the missionaries to fear for their lives. They knew the power of the gospel and what the sharing of that message of God's redeeming love had accomplished in the hearts of hundreds of Africans. They constantly felt the pressure of "so little time and so much to do."

The Central African Republic early welcomed Red Communist China to come and help. The president, Dako, acknowledged some of the possible dangers, but that his hands were tied, as this little country was so far inland and surrounded by bigger countries that had already joined hands with China. These other countries could cut off all supplies to the country of CAR. One of BMM couples was invited to dinner at President Dako's home, and they had a real good talk together about the future of the country. Everyone was concerned because as soon as the door was open to them, China immediately sent one hundred people to that little country.

Workers Desperately Needed

"O where, O where were the missionaries who would come and care to help open blind eyes to the wonderful truths of God." Workers were needed once things had quieted down after independence. At that time, Baptist Mid-Missions had already been in that country for forty-four years, and the total number of missionaries as yet had not reached one hundred. They earnestly prayed that the Christians in the USA would have an increased burden to pray and send them some help.

Nearly everyone on the Bangassou station was due for furlough the next year, after four to five years serving the Lord in the tropics, with its heat and many diseases. Their calling, plus the real love and close fellowship with their dear Africans didn't urge them to take furloughs, but good sense told them that they needed to get some rest and medical attention. As soon as they arrived back in the United States, physical exams, including lots of necessary lab work, (everyone has more than one little foreigner living in them to slow them down and destroy the body) would be on the program, followed by the necessary treatments. It is often said that as tune ups for vehicles are in order to keep them running effectively, even so, our bodies need to be taken care of. The missionaries are the vehicles God uses to carry the gospel to a needy and dying world.

Full Hands

Once again, sorrow struck the mission village. Tuesday morning, Ndegue, one of our Bible school students, reported that his wife was quite ill. Dr. Saethers, one of the Congo refugees, was called to see her and had scheduled more extensive exams for her on Thursday morning. But because the doctor fell ill, the missionaries took her to the local hospital at the post, and the doctor there removed a fibroid tumor. She had postoperative complications and hemorrhaged to death that evening. The next day, she was buried in the little cemetery behind the mission village. She was such a sweet and happy Christian, but the Lord saw fit to take her home to heaven. Her husband, Ndegue, a second year Bible school student, still had two more years to finish, and normally students had to be married to become a student in the Bible school, but he was permitted to finish. As heartless as it might seem in other cultures, this was a wise protection for the student and necessary for harmony in their little mission village. Immorality was a way of life, and rampantly practiced among the non-Christians in that land. If the Christians were not really dedicated and obedient to the Lord, it became a real problem. A single man had pressure from so many around him to get his own wife or to take the one already married to someone else. Naturally, this was one more request for prayer as the prayer letters went back to the churches and people back home.

Being a generous and hospitable people, as soon as the chicken pox visited their village, it became a visitor in every home in the mission village. Dear Ruth had her hands full trying to minister to the other medical needs of so many people, and when an epidemic such as this struck, they all cried to God for added strength for her and others who were ministering day and night to these hurting people. With epidemics come added deaths, thus the additional fatigue is not only physical, but emotional. All of the missionaries took turns holding babies and ministering to so many grieving people. Doris was weary, but fully aware that her fatigue was much less than that of Ruth. Ruth's weariness included many medical decisions for each case, which were often accompanied by hideous screams.

There were so many little folks who needed loving care. For instance, little two-year old Etienne was hovering between life and death for a number of weeks. His illness began with a severe case of chicken pox, followed by whooping cough, malaria, and anemia from hookworm infection. One leg became quite lifeless, possibly

118

due to the many injections he received. This is one example of daily treating about 200 people; then the mumps started to make its rounds, especially among the children. Their hands were full.

"Mademoiselle, Gueret Jumped!"

Many unplanned events came their way. On one occasion, Doris was driving back from town with more building provisions for their house; they had waiting literally months and years for the time and help to replace the tumble down house that they had been living in for many years. Two boys from the mission village were at the post and asked for a lift back home. While driving through the mission village and nearly home, Gueret, one of the teenage boys, decided to jump out of the moving truck. The other boy tried to stop him but to no avail, and he started pounding on the roof of the cab of the truck, yelling, "Miss, Miss—Gueret jumped and he is lying in the middle of the road!" Doris stopped and there was Gueret sprawled on the road like a corpse. He was rushed to the hospital at the post and the French doctor worked on him for quite awhile. He was seriously injured and was unconscious most of the time for several days. Many of the morning classes that morning turned into prayer meetings for Gueret.

Doris was very upset and crying. The students prayed that this trial would not weigh her down and make her weary of the Lord's calling. Many of the Christians came to sympathize with them and to pray for their heavy hearts. Their sincere concern was a source of help and comfort to her. Two weeks went by before Gueret could eat and recognize people. Then, he even sang and talked some. The call went out for continued prayer as he was still unable to walk.

Bet Ta Ouali: Our Faithful Women Conference

Over six hundred women gathered at Bangassou for the Faithful Women's conference, and it was such an uplifting joy to one and all. Many of them walked sixty to seventy miles to get to the mission where the conference was held. This was part of the same organization that Doris and two other ladies had organized for their entire field. The purpose was to encourage the women to share their faith in Christ with other women in the villages and markets. Little had been done to encourage these women to know that they had great worth in God's eyes. In some ways, Doris had the advantage in starting this ministry for the women over some of the other areas of the country, and the men on her station as well as the leaders in the local church appreciated the encouragement for the African women.

With all the uproar and problems in the governments in other countries around them, they particularly looked to the Lord for a God-honoring procedure and means to communicate with the government that this was not an anti-government program. On the last day of the Faithful Women's conference, they marched to the local government offices singing the national anthem, plus a song to uplift the name of Christ written especially for their group, as a testimony of their love for God. It was impressive to see even the older women marching along with their canes and keeping step. Doris didn't use a cane but she felt like she could use one after that little hike of about seven miles. At another date, when the President came for a visit, the local Faithful Women marched out to the field where the plane landed and sang the national anthem there, too. He shook hands with each of the ladies. Doris jokingly said that she wasn't sure she should ever wash her hand; "After all, have you ever shaken hands with a president?"

The House—Can it Really Be True?

Finally, their house was on the way up. Mr. Nimmo came three weeks before in early March, 1965, and poured the cement for the termite course all the way around the foundation and now about seventy-five percent of the walls are up to two to three feet. The termite course is a cement slab on which the walls are built. You might call it a roadblock. This is to waylay the termites in their travels up the walls and to the roof. It helps some. Three doorframes also were set in place. So much work had to proceed with very little supervision of the workmen.

Doris came home between classes one day to check on a wall that they were building. "Whoops, you will have to start over," she said. The wall was leaning so that she wondered if they used a picture of the Tower of Pisa as their pattern. She then showed them with the use of the plumb line how much the wall was leaning.

They said," We had to do it that way as the plum line wouldn't hang straight the way we wanted it to do." It sounds funny unless you are trying to build a house. "What would she know," they must've thought, "she was a woman?" How would you answer that one?

Doris suggested, "Why don't you check with one of the men for a second opinion before you go any farther?" She knew that the men were all so busy, and even though one and all were concerned about getting the house done, it might be a problem to find them with a few extra minutes, that is when they weren't occupied with several other things that needed attention.

Could it be real? The house that they had talked about rebuilding for the last few years was finally in the process. The need had been there for some time, but the overly full program didn't allow for adding much time to that project, too. Then too, the girls were gone to classes and the dispensary so much of the time that it didn't take first place in list of needs. After all, didn't they have mosquito nets over the beds to protect them from the snakes, mice, bugs, and grass that fell from the roof to disturb their sleep? And it even helped a lot to hinder the mosquitoes from annoying them.

They purchased cement from across the river when it was available and it was safe to go for it. Due to the inland transport and lack of good trucking from point A to point B in CAR, the cement coming from down country often had become concrete before arriving at its destination. There were no home improvement stores or any other possible place to obtain materials within hundreds of miles from their station. Over the years they had collected some of the materials on hand. They had already purchased the windows from a missionary who wouldn't be returning to the field. Many months earlier, the aluminum for the roof had been purchased and trucked in. The bricks had been made and burned in a kiln. Mr. Nimmo was willing to come from Ouango from time to time to help and oversee the building, and the men on the station could and would give a hand occasionally as their time permitted. More refugees from the Congo had arrived and Mr. Hansen helped supervise some of the work on the house before they left for Norway. "How about wood for framing doors, windows, making walls, constructing A-Beams for the roof, and so forth?" Some screws, nails and hardware for assembling might be found at the local post, but one didn't count on that. Maybe they could find what they needed in someone's toolbox, or in the barrels in their storeroom. Yes, of great necessity, they all had barrels and they all had storerooms.

Missionaries going home on furlough needed to store personal things away from the termites and the thieves. The houses they lived in, if they had one, needed to be vacated easily for others to move in. Furniture was shared by all. At Bangassou, they had some good carpenters who knew how to make beautiful furniture with the red mahogany wood that was available.

The storerooms provided the resident missionaries somewhere safe to put the supplies they had brought for their four to five year terms. Mothers brought schoolbooks, clothing, shoes, and so forth to use for their children as they grew and were needed. Many ladies' groups from churches in the States made many nice things to give as award gifts to the Africans. Foodstuffs that would keep such as soda, baking powder, seasonings, as well as many other items that could not be purchased there were stored in the barrels to be used as needed. By experience they learned not to pack cake mixes, puddings, and other edibles in the same barrel as perfumed items such as soap; imagine a cake flavored with Lifebuoy soap. Many ladies' groups in our supporting churches made up crafts, clothing, baby garments, and the like, and these were they kept in the barrels until needed. You see, the termites aren't picky eaters. They couldn't chew the metal of the barrels, so that wasn't on their diet, but just give them a little crack that wasn't sealed well and they were busy at work.

The girls always carried one or two layettes in the glove compartment of the truck. These were especially needed out on the road trips for the unscheduled baby deliveries. One ladies' group made up about fifty headscarves for awards for the girls in the children's classes. Their custom called for little girls to wear something on their heads, even if they had but little covering on their bodies. Therefore, much nice children's clothing was also part of the baggage in the barrels, and was so appreciated.

Bangui, Here We Come Again!

On the nineteenth of January, Ruth started out once again for Bangui at 5 a.m. with the Peugeot to take the Norwegian missionaries to Bangui to catch a plane. As usual, some Africans also went along with her to help her if needed. Doris left at 6 a.m. with the Chevrolet pickup truck, some more of the Norwegian Baptist missionaries, some Africans who were with her, and plenty of baggage. Ruth proceeded quite well until about thirty miles from Bangui, when the front of the Peugeot dropped to the ground. It took a while for Doris to get that far with the Chevrolet, as she had to spend a day at the garage at Bambari on the way down. The dear Chevy had to go back to the garage again at Bangui upon their arrival there.

Giving Thanks Continually

Afterwards, Doris gave thanks for all this in a prayer letter: "How do we give thanks for all of this?" We all arrived safely; the Lord made it possible for Ruth to get the Peugeot fixed and sold; in less than two weeks, they had a pleasant, non eventful trip back to Bangassou and the dear people excitedly welcomed them back in their midst; the meetings in Bangui were profitable. God honored and encouraged those working with the "Teens" and the "Faithful Women" through the ministry of His servants; Miss Thora, one of the Norwegian missionaries, remained in Bangassou to care for the dispensary in Ruth's absence; Doris received a package from home with a pair of badly-needed shoes that were exactly her size, and most importantly, knowing that many people back home were praying for us, we thank Him."

Persecution, Killings, Oppression, and Bloodshed Continues Across the River in the Former Belgian Congo

Doris wrote in a prayer letter: "Many of our fellow missionaries are still there in spite of the American-Belgian Rescue Mission that has been formed. Hunger, persecutions and massacres continue among the Africans as well as among the missionaries that had come from several countries to share the gospel message to the Africans. As this was happening, the Holtes were still in the Congo as prisoners. They were taken from their station to another station farther away from the river transport to make it more difficult for them to escape across the river to freedom. Once the Holtes eventually escaped, they came to the Bangassou station and were both a big help in the work there, as were all of the Norwegian missionaries who were refugees at Bangassou. Some were with them as long as ten months. They hated to believe that they weren't going back to their ministry in the Congo. God turned their heartaches and sorrows into an expulsion of enormous help for the work and ministry at Bangassou. One example out of many of their dedication occurred one day as Doris was holding reading class down the hill at the church around one o'clock. While teaching, she fell unconscious to the ground. The Africans brought her up the hill to another missionary's home, which was about a fifteen minute walk away. She was still oblivious to what was going on around her. Mrs. Holte, a nurse, tried in vain for several minutes before she could get a pulse. She and her husband both sat beside Doris for hours checking her vitals and praying for her life. Heat and fatigue were deemed the culprits in what they defined as a heat stroke."

Projects for the Year for Bangassou Station

Progress in the African church there continued as outlined in another prayer letter:

"Building of at least thirty permanent houses, required by the government, for Bible school students:

Missionary Project

Building of African Pastor's house:
African Church Project

Completion of church building here on the station:
African Church project

Building a Church building on the other side of town:
African Church project

Completion of African Pastor's house on the other side of town: African Church project

Building Nephew/Gilbert house: Missionary project
Bible school classes, twenty-two hours weekly:
Chasteens, Townes', Ruth and Doris

Children's classes: Doris and African helpers

Teenage girls: Ruth, Doris, and African helpers

Teenage boys: Ruth and African helpers

Teacher's classes: Gene Townes, African Pastors, and students

Class at French School: Gene Townes

Release time classes in schools: Viola Brown, Bible school students and wives

Church services, prayer meeting, and new converts class: African pastors and helpers.

Men and women's reading classes:
Doris, African pastors, and helpers

Children's Sunday school and Jr. Church:
Bible school students

Dispensary: Ruth, Thora, and African helpers.

Bible Book store: Dean Chasteen and African assistant.

Entertainment of guests: Everybody

Boys' Brigade and Pioneer girls:
Ruth, Viola, African helpers and leaders."

One Saturday, when they didn't have classes, Ruth and Doris, went with the teenage girls to dig out a pile of sand to be used in the student housing. While Ruth got redder in the sun, Doris got browner. They both enjoyed the girls and did lots of laughing together, which was good therapy for all of them. They were used of the Lord to minister to the girls by their lives and their lips.

All in a Day's Work: A Wedding

With Ruth's shoes, Doris' necklace, a party dress from one of Ruth's barrels of used clothing which needed a bit of altering, and mosquito netting worked up for a veil, the bride was ready for the one of the first African Christian weddings, as they were usually arranged between families. Ruth sat in the back of the church to help the bride get down the aisle, and Doris was up front playing the accordion and rejoicing as one more Christian couple desired to establish a home with Christ as the Lord of their lives. As they continued to hold the children and teenage classes, their prayer to God was that they might be able to teach Christian principles to the young people so that eventually their desire would be to have homes and families that glorified the Lord Jesus.

Dean Chasteen had not been feeling well for a few months, so they decided to take their furlough a bit early. On their departure in May, both sides of the mission road were lined up with our dear, Christian believers showering the Chasteens with flowers as they drove off of the station. During that month, Thora Hoyskel, a refugee from the Congo who had been with us for ten months also left to go back to Norway, and Viola Brown left for furlough. Gene and Marion Townes, along with Ruth and Doris, were the only remaining missionaries on the station before Lester and Martha Fogle later came to fill in as the head of the station. Their schedule was so full and they looked to the Lord for added strength each day. He had promised, "As your days are so shall your strength be." He was faithful in every way. They felt so blessed to be His sent ones.

Their temporary housing required lots of pans and buckets, especially in the kitchen, to collect the coffee-colored rain. But the good news was that their new house kept going up and the aluminum roof could soon be added by fall. They just didn't have much time to think about the housing, with all the activities, classes, and the dispensary for Ruth with up to 200 patients per day, but it would be a hallelujah day when they were in the house that had been in the process of being built for so long.

One might sometimes wonder how they made out without a vehicle in the early years. The positive side was that, they weren't paying ten dollars a gallon for gasoline, except when they borrowed the truck. Well, they weren't called Pollyannas for nothing. Besides the running to camps and conferences, the little green Chevy truck was frequently used for ambulance and hearse service. One Friday morning, Doris took a lady who was having a difficult labor in to the French hospital at the post. She died during the night, so as soon as Ruth got back from the youth camp, Lester took the truck and went to get the body. Then on a Sunday about two o'clock, the message came from the village that one of the Bible school students was in labor. Ruth took her to the hospital, but before she returned they brought in a woman who had been attacked by evil spirits, and before Ruth had finished trying to help her, word came that there was someone with a strangulated hernia in a neighboring village; so off they went to get the patient and transport him to the hospital at the post. Then the next morning at dawn, Doris left for the Faithful Women's conference at an outstation. She came back rejoicing as she shared how the Holy Spirit had worked in hearts of the women at that conference.

Annual Field Conference for Baptist Mid-Missions

The annual field conference, which included travelling over five hundred miles of very bad roads, was almost upon them. It was a joy to be with others with a mutual burden and joy in the work, but the tiresome two day trip was not anticipated with great joy. Not only were they sure to tear up some tires, break springs on the truck and be exhausted with the heat, they had no air conditioning, and because it was dry, they all had a coat of dust and looked as though they had changed nationality before arriving at their destination. The rewards of this long trip were many: fellowship in the Word of God, sharing burdens and blessings, enjoying special music, singing God's praises together, listening to special music from their gifted co-workers who they saw and heard from only once a year. All of this was the reviving that they needed to go back to the varied ministries at the various stations where God had placed them. Blessings and problems awaited them, but the inner man was happily fortified to anticipate with joy the future ministry God had waiting for them as they returned to their stations.

Help Comes Indirectly from the USA

For several months now they had been able to get some American government surplus milk from the French hospital at the post. Every Tuesday, Thursday and Saturday, they had fifty to sixty children in the milk line. It was a hit with most of the children, and fun to watch them enjoy their milk and come back in line a second time for more. They were very grateful to the Lord, to the American government, and the French hospital for this means of ministering to physical needs of these little ones, even if it was only for a few months' time. There were three little emaciated ones who especially needed the milk, but they had to be coaxed and bribed to drink it. Their hearts were often sad due to the evidence of hunger and depravity that they constantly witnessed.

Hungry Not Only for Physical Food, but for God's Food, His Word

"But Miss, I have to have a New Testament. You've got to sell me a New Testament." Doris had taken eighteen New Testaments in the Sango language with her to the "Faithful Women's" conference out in one of the bush villages. In just a few minutes after her arrival, even before she could unload other things from the truck for the three-day conference, all the New Testaments had been sold. "I wish I had some more with me but I don't have even one left to sell to you," she told them. Upon hearing these words, one lady sat down with her head in her hands; her body literally shook as she sobbed and sobbed because there were no Testaments left for her to buy. Doris was happy and sad simultaneously. Glad for the desire and hunger for God's Word, mixed with regret that it took so many years to get the New Testament translated and transported to them in the middle of Africa. Once again, Doris was reminded of the need to pray for transport of the copies of the scriptures that were waiting down country. As these dear people learned to read, they eagerly saved their *patas* (least valuable pieces of money) in order to have God's book all for their own. Repeatedly, they had to answer, "We have no more left," as the dear ones came with their coins to buy their own copy.

In the children's class, Doris rewarded the kids for memorizing verses from the Bible. On one occasion three of the children stood before the congregation and recited seventy-two verses with their references and without prompting. The delight on their faces when the reward of a New Testament was presented to each of them was a picture that she would never forget. One of them was eight-year old Germain, who attended children's classes faithfully and is now a doctor Bordeaux, France. He and his wife are faithful witnesses to this day and workers in one of the mission churches there. God graciously allows Doris to see him each trip she takes to Bordeaux. What a joy to know that there will be hundreds and hundreds that she'll meet in glory because of their hunger for God and His Word.

How our hearts praise Him for so many of God's faithful servants who spent years in getting the Word into the Sango language. Mr. Haas, the forerunner and founder of BMM was a linguist. He translated and distributed portions of scriptures into the Sango trade language almost immediately upon arrival in that country. There were many tribal languages across that area of the world called French Equatorial Africa. Once again, we see the evidence of how this man of God listened to God's directions in this very important matter of translating Scripture and hymns into the Sango trade language. Psalm 119:130 says, "The entrance of Thy word giveth light. It giveth understanding unto the simple." Now more people could know about God's Son and His love for them in a common language. In southern Chad, Sango was used for years and is still, in spite of the many tribal languages that now have the scriptures. This was one form of glue that helped hold the tribes and country together during all of the changes at the time of their independence, and led to unity between tribes because they could communicate. The general consensus among many was that much of the trouble across the river in the former Belgian Congo was due to multiple tribal languages and no trade language, thus little communication between tribes was possible. Because of the burden and insight of one man, plus the steadfastness of a language committee, the entire word of God in the Sango language was in the hands of God's servants and their African brothers and sisters. It doesn't stop there. The Brethren mission that worked in the Western part of the country had worked on the same Sango language committee with BMM and all of that area profited from the same Sango Bible.

Perilous Times

"For such a time as this" was the theme of their yearly mission conference held at Fort Crampel, which was renamed Kagabandoro shortly after independence. The Lord was honored and the missionaries experienced a real oneness during the conference. They could all see the dire need for missionaries on all the stations. As they left that conference they rejoiced over the privilege of being soldiers and fighting the same battle to honor the name of the Lord. The urgency of the hour was imprinted on every heart. Little did they know or even dream, that in just a few short years, all but one of those stations would have no resident missionary.

"Old soldiers never die, they just fade away," was a quote by a military man many years ago. Unless you read history books, many of those old soldiers who had a part in our freedom are unknown. This is also true of God's soldiers. The message of freedom that they shared is what has blessed the Central African Republic and many other countries around the world by God's grace as they continue to share the same message with their own people. Doris has often prayed and wept for those countries and stations where our gracious God allowed an unknown country girl to have full hands as she shared the everlasting message of God's grace that Jesus saves. Because of the obedience of God's children, some of every tribe and nation have, and will continue to enjoy, the riches of heaven.

Doris stopped at Bangui in the Central African Republic on her way home for a rest and to share with the churches and people who had prayed and supported her in so many ways. Many heads of state from other African countries were in Bangui to greet and receive the Chinese who had an exposition in the capital city. The Chinese were there to represent and explain how wonderful it was to be a communist country. Knowing how poor these countries were in material things, the missionaries were heavy hearted at the thought that they could be easily impressed and tempted by communist rule.

Like many other colonies, the government of France had recently granted their independence. The missionaries felt the urgency to protect their God-given African family by their prayers. The headlines in a local paper in the United States read, *"Missionary Tells of Red Peril in Darkest Africa."*

Shortly after Doris had arrived back in the United States, the Elmira Star Gazette asked for an interview. The reporter came to the house to get a report on the situation in her area of Africa. Even then, Doris didn't feel it would be advisable to share any news that could endanger the missionaries and the dear African family who was still there. She was happy to tell them the real reason that missionaries were still living and working in that under-privileged area of the world. It was difficult to explain why they counted it a privilege to be God's ambassadors to a people that were eager to hear about Him in the center of that continent.

Furlough: Rest, Reporting to Praying People, and Healing

In Africa, the missionaries had worked up a system of codes that had been brought back by furloughing missionaries. From these codes they shared urgent needs with many praying people by way of prayer letters. Thus, as they sent letters home and vice versa, they could add a sentence or two using the code words to help others know how to pray for them. This assured people of their safety. They could also share a bit of the real situation of events. This was a comfort to family and friends back home, because the unknown is often much more strenuous on the nerves.

The recommended term on the field was approximately four years. As for all missionaries at that time, the wise and required process by the mission agency was for them to have medical check-ups shortly after arriving back in the United States. This included the regular physicals, dental work, and any special needs that they knew about. As has been mentioned earlier, usually those coming out of the tropics had experienced several bouts of malaria, filaria and other maladies that needed follow-up attention.

As a rule, Doris scheduled meetings near her home in Pennsylvania shortly after arriving home. By the time summer arrived, she was booked up as missionary speaker in three churches for vacation Bible school, which ran for two weeks each back then, plus one week each for four different youth camps. Before returning to Africa, she drove to the west coast from Pennsylvania to speak in supporting churches in Washington, California, and Nevada.

Late that summer, a trip to the mission doctor and the hospital in Cleveland was scheduled for a physical and minor surgery in preparation for returning to Africa in a few weeks. A large, possibly cancerous tumor caused a few changes of plans. Major surgery was required followed by a month of rest and recuperation in Cleveland. Many ministered to her during that time, including her dear niece Karen, who flew out to Cleveland to care for her and drive her back home, even though her own wedding was about a month away. The report of no cancer found was another big plus in that adventure.

Cries for Help!

"Miss, won't you hurry back to help us?" Don't leave us without our Mama any longer, please." Right after celebrating Christmas at home with their families, Doris and Ruth were on their way back to Africa and to their second family there. As they drove in to the mission, God's dear ones lined the road waving flowers, singing, and welcoming them back. It didn't take long to be back in the buzz and battle for the Lord. Eggs, pineapples, peanuts, and bananas were some of the welcome gifts that were placed on the veranda of their house that was in the process of being built. Ruth lived with the Fogles and Doris lived with Elda Long until at least part of the new house was completed.

There was another urgent need that would likely take precedence. Their student village needed permanent housing. There was a requirement by the government to replace all of the mud huts in the student village. Two more foundations had been laid for student houses. The government's threats to destroy the temporary housing seemed to appear more and more imminent. Not just time and helpers were needed, but also the funds to buy the materials. The missionaries didn't have a building fund, other than funds from home that were designated for that project. Consequently, they tightened their belts and built the houses from personal funds.

Ruth and Doris Finally Move into Their New Home

No, it wasn't completely finished but it was livable, and they could keep working on it as they had time. Doris came from a family of builders. In a letter home to her dad, Doris wrote, "This morning, about ten, I finished nailing the last piece of lath on the ceiling in the guest room and Dorothy Moon arrived at 5 p.m. to live with us for a few months." What fun it had been trying to get the lath to fit. Unfortunately, the masons who had built the walls were specialists in ignoring plumb lines. She thought that she would save time, in lieu of someone eventually being able to help her. So she carefully measured the floor, which she thought was equal in size to the ceiling. Then she cut the necessary pieces so that they only needed nailing in place, but the uneven, wavy spots on the walls didn't agree to her plan. With whittling and cutting, the ceiling was completed and the florescent light installed in time for Dorothy's arrival. Doris told Ruth that if any of her brothers or Dad, whose business was building houses, could have seen the process, they would have had a lot of chuckles.

She knew that any one of them would have been frustrated with the lack of supplies and delays they would have had to face on a regular basis. Needless to say, the girls knew that their main desire and purpose for being in Africa was not to be too concerned about living conditions.

Why Do Missionaries Go to Those Dark Countries?

Only God's Word in the hearts and lives of any people group can work miracles. Sayo had recently given his life to the Lord, and when he died, his Christian funeral was very different from that of his father Bangassou. There was lots of singing, praying, and praising God that Sayo was now in glory. When Bangassou had died, his favorite wife was killed and buried with him. As was the custom, several others were killed and buried around Bangassou's grave, supposedly to protect him. About one hundred other wives were killed and eaten at the feast that followed his funeral. Bangassou had not heard the gospel, and he died without Christ as his Savior. Sayo had heard and believed the gospel message not only with his ears but also with his heart. No one was killed at the time of his death. There was much singing and rejoicing because the Christians knew that their chief had gone to join the greatest of all chiefs, Jesus.

Viola Brown Comes for a Short-term Visit

Viola had a little French two horsepower jitney. That means that there wasn't much power unless they were pushing. They drove it to an outstation to minister because it used much less gas than the pick-up truck. Not a good decision! Nearly every little hill or knoll needed extra horsepower to make it up the grade. As if the heat and bad roads weren't sufficient problems, pushing that car just added discomfort and fatigue. They were smart enough to leave it at home and spend more money on gas for the truck for the following trips, although they did enjoy some real laughs with their escapades.

Bibles, Bibles, Bibles!

A shipment of 800 Bibles arrived at their station from down country. Everyone was so excited. This would be only a beginning to fulfill the demand of the people for the whole Word of God. The New Testament had been in their hands for several years, but now they had the whole Bible. Those who knew how to read, and were able to buy a Bible, paid a small percentage of the actual cost. They became so wrapped up in reading its pages that other activities had to stop. Doris was delighted and praising God that the Bibles has arrived before the Faithful Women's conference that was scheduled to begin almost immediately. She had prepared tracts, Bibles, and the necessary medical equipment for her trip in the morning.

Doris was supposed to be on her way at 4 a.m., but was delayed by illness until 5 a.m. for the Faithful Women's conference at an outstation. The first session for the women from ten outstation churches was scheduled for 7 a.m. It was raining hard, and Doris was ill when she arrived at the ferry that would take her across the river. That's when the trouble started. The fellows who manned the ferry told her that the exit on the other end of the crossing was too slippery to drive the car off the ferry and up the grade. She told them that normally that was true, but she wouldn't know for sure unless she tried. She was going for God, and He had the power to get her up that slippery, impossible slope if He willed it so. After 1½ hours of trying to persuade them, they were willing to try. Not surprisingly, she was up the hill on the other side without a problem, and although she arrived at the conference late, she did arrive.

"Go with God," was an expression repeatedly used and experienced. The grass roof wasn't on the house yet where Doris would be staying for three nights. They worked all day, and that night completed the roof on the new house that she occupied for the conference. After the evening service, they asked her if she would like water to take a bath. After she gave an affirmative answer, they arrived with a basin about thirty-six inches across filled with water, and put it in the main room in the middle of the floor. When she asked where she would take her bath, they said, "Isn't this all right?" With ten men and women in the room, she thought, "Lord, what do I do now?" After she hesitated for awhile, the men left and the women pushed the pan of water over in the corner. They were probably thinking, "These white people are so funny." Well, the little kerosene lantern didn't give much light, and she was sure that they saw nothing amiss in the arrangement. Often it was suggested to the missionaries that to best understand the people they must think African, but there are exceptions, as you can see.

The second day of the conference everything started on schedule and all was going well, until the pastor ran in and said, "Miss, can you come quickly? One of the ladies is in hard labor at my house." Doris dashed to the house, scrubbed her hands, situated the mother-to-be on a grass mat on the ground, and shortly the attendance at the conference increased by one. A sweet little baby girl had joined the ranks. When they asked Doris to name the baby, she named it Lucille after her first co-worker. They let her know that wasn't what they meant. "We want one of your names," they said. "Take your pick," Doris suggested, thinking that the name Gilbert in French can be used for either a boy (Gilbert) or a girl (Gilberte). Instead, they chose the name Doris for their baby daughter. This occasioned the name to be used repeatedly as she helped in many deliveries.

The pastor gave a terrific message on Sunday morning before the ladies started the trek back to their villages, many carrying burdens in their hearts and on their heads. "The distance between God and me is great. Pray that I'll learn to walk real close," said one of the ladies as she was leaving. Many of these ladies were beaten daily by their unsaved, drunken husbands, or by his second or third wife. Even as they would travel to come to the conferences, the soldiers were along the road waiting to molest them. With written permission from one of the local officials, Doris made up permits, and mimeographed multiple copies to be signed by their pastors. The ladies carried these permits to show to the soldiers who attempted to stop them. It is possible that the soldiers couldn't even read, but it looked official enough for them to allow them to go by unmolested. Doris loved these ladies very much, and she was glad to listen, sympathize, pray, and try with understanding to care about each one and their problems.

Problems? A group of seven women who all had unsaved husbands came together from one village. Very likely, each had been beaten and misused daily by their husband or some of his other wives. For them to come to a conference required a great deal of leaning on the Lord for strength that only God can give. In any conversation that Doris had with them, as they exposed their suffering and heartache, they always asked for prayer that their husbands would come to Jesus, too. They would often make the two or three-day walk with their little ones tied on to their backs or cradled in their arms. They experienced no love or consideration except in their relationship with the Lord Jesus.

Even local authorities were beginning to see the changes in lives in their local precincts. These godly women shared God's Word, not only by word but also by caring deeds and righteous living. Some of those in government tried to encourage the leaders to leave the business of winning souls by offering them money. God's way isn't always sought; instead they desire to honor themselves and profit from their positions.

The Central African Republic had been one of the most receptive and fruitful countries to the message of God's Word on the continent of Africa. At that time, Baptist Mid-Missions had just two couples in residence there. They were constantly traveling east and west, north and south over deplorable and dangerous roads, to encourage and help God's servants and people in their walk with the Lord and to see the unsaved accept the message of deliverance and peace. Bandits, broken bridges, broken vehicles, tropical climate, and diseases didn't hinder them from keeping on with the gospel message. Ask them if they considered it a life of sacrificial hardship.

Are You Ready for the Next Exciting Trip?

Ruth Nephew, Dorothy Moon, Viola Brown and Doris packed the truck and took a three-day trip to Obo to visit missionaries from the Africa Inland Mission. Obo is located nearly in the corner where the Central African Republic, Zaire, and Sudan come together. They had four ferry crossings, only one flat tire, and true to form, a few stops with engine trouble. Doris was the mechanic who got the truck to purring (with a cough). Then each time it became breathless and died, Doris would check her huge mechanics book to see if she could revive it by playing with some other part of the motor when it decided to rest a bit. The other three took walks, picked flowers, and patiently waited for the old truck to make another hop. A trek to an old cave was among the adventures, but they didn't find any of the ivory and guns that were supposed to have been placed there by an old chief.

Their trip became even more eventful as they traveled on to Bambouti, located on the border of the Sudan. Even back in 1968, that area was heavily patrolled. Several Sudanese who lived close to the border had been killed, and a camp for 20,000 Sudanese refugees had been set up across the border in the Central African Republic. As they traveled close to the border, they found a large military truck carrying soldiers stopped in the middle of the road. The missionaries cleared a path through the jungle with machetes to go around the truck. On their return down the same road about 8 p.m., they found that the truck had been parked on a bridge and the soldiers had gone to bed. Mr. Lindquist, an Africa Inland Mission missionary stationed at Obo who had joined them for the trek looked around until he found the soldiers. With much persuasion, he convinced them to get up and push the truck off the bridge. Unfortunately, they left it in the middle of the road on the other side of the bridge. Thus the jungle cutters went to work again to cut another road around the truck and continued on their way.

Teachers Needed

"Me, teach the books of the minor prophets in Bible school?" exclaimed Doris. The station at Bangassou was faced with a classroom of future pastors, but few missionaries to fill the teaching positions. There was only one man left on the station at that time, and he couldn't teach all of the classes. So Corky did her best. (Doris was called Corky because she filled holes in the program here and there). At least they had the whole Bible in the Sango language, thus facilitating the assignment. Nevertheless, there were still all the class notes to prepare. These were written and then reproduced on the old mimeograph machine. It had already worked hard making hundreds of turns in preparing materials for other classes, especially for the children. She chuckled often as she gained insights and witticisms from her studies, usually from 4 a.m. to 6 a.m., in preparation for her class that started at 6:30 a.m. She was also teaching French, Missions, Child Evangelism and math, but nothing rejoiced her heart as much as the study and teaching of the Minor Prophets. She taught the early class because she had children's classes scheduled from 8:30 to 10:30 each morning.

Outstation, here we come again. Traveling on a road not usually used for vehicles, they got stuck in the mud, as usual. They repeatedly tried to advance by digging out the sod and filling the holes with stones. "That ought to take care of it; let's try it now," they yelled. The driver stepped on the gas and the accelerator said, "I'm resting for awhile." As they pondered the next step to take, a big truck loaded with men came along. It took about an hour of persuasion until the men heard Doris say, "Well, I guess we'll just have to sleep out here in the jungle tonight, but then we are used to it." That helped the men decide that they shouldn't make the white people do that, and they said, "Maybe we can do something." One of the advantages of getting stuck in the jungle was that they were able to cut down a tree to make a twenty-foot pole. They cut notches in each end to hook on to the bumpers. The pole was then tied in place with inner tube string. Inner tube string was old inner tubes cut into long rubber bands. Doris just *happened* to have an old inner tube. She *happened* to have a machete to cut the pole. The truck just *happened* to be there, even though vehicles didn't travel that road. Don't you believe it; God planned it all. The girls were able to witness to a truckload of men about Jesus and His love, and the reason why they were on that road at that time. How great to know that the Lord orders the steps of His servants! When they had been pulled out of the mud, the starter said, "Ok, let's go." The other truck backed up to a path so the girls could go by, and they journeyed on to another women's conference in the bush country. Needless to say, they sought another way back home.

More Filariasis

As mentioned earlier, filaria was a common malady. At one point, Doris was so well covered with sores where the filaria had built their homes all over her body that one of the older nurses told her that she was pretty sure that she had leprosy. Contracting leprosy had been the one thing that she feared the most when she knew that God was calling her to that continent. When she had first arrived in Africa, she had to chuckle when the very first person with whom she shook hands in Bangassou had no fingers because she was a leper.

Don't you love God's sense of humor? No, she didn't have leprosy, but she did get a bad scolding from the French doctor whom she finally went to see after two weeks. The large festered bunch on her lower back was carbuncles, called *anthrax* in French, with nests of little filarial soldiers surrounding it, thus making the whole situation critical.

Christmas, Again

The Christmas program was two and a half hours long with about 2,000 people attending. Two men accepted Christ that day. Ask the Africans, "Why such a long program?" Their reply would be, "We are celebrating the birth of a King!"

Christmas Dinner! Throughout the year, as they received something special from home or something unusual someone found when they took a trip to Bangui, they would set it aside for this special dinner. The Golikes, who were now manning the work in the Bangassou/Ouango area, hosted the meal. There were thirteen of them, including five children, and Bob's sister and family who traveled down from Chad. They had found some fresh butter and cheese, which they brought along. Their menu consisted of chicken, gravy, oyster stuffing, mashed potatoes made from a package, succotash, canned corn from the United States, beans raised in Africa, home-made rolls (nothing different there, as they made all their bread), gelatin salad, squash pie, and ice cream made with the hand-turned freezer. Each one made all the ice they possibly could make in their kerosene refrigerators to have enough to turn the ice cream freezer. Another special treat was popcorn that was made into caramel corn to eat later in the day.

"Miss, Pastor Togbiambi's wife is in labor and has been since last night." It was Christmas morning, and in the rush of getting everything in order for the children's program, she decided that a trip to the hospital needed to be fitted into the day's activities. Otherwise, she might be delivering a baby during the program. Incidentally, Doris delivered this lady's tenth child only a few minutes after she arrived at their home.

Someone's at the Door

"Cough, cough," was the Africans' way of knocking.

"Who's there?"

"It is Manda."

"What are the words on your heart?" Doris asked.

"A woman in the village is in labor. Can Miss come and take her to the hospital?" he replied. She delivered the baby five minutes after arriving.

On a different occasion, "Miss, my wife is eight months pregnant, but now there is an animal eating in her body, and it is hurting way up her back. Will you come?" The "animal" was labor pains, and a baby boy arrived at the same time that Doris did.

Soon after that, "Miss, please take my wife to the hospital. Her baby has sought in vain for a way to arrive." Because the baby was almost there, they took the bamboo bed and all, and left for the hospital. Doris delivered the baby on the way. Many times Doris practiced her amateur midwifery skills on the back of the truck for those mothers who waited too long.

"Miss, the pastor's wife needs to go to the hospital because her baby is working her. Can you come quickly and take her?" They arrived in plenty of time for this one. All of this happened in six days time in the schedule of a non-medical missionary: "ambulance services anyone?"

Mechanic Needed

As they went to their field conference that year, another eventful trip was in store for them. Since the Nimmos traveled with them, everyone took their turn riding in the back of the pick-up. Other than the carburetor, distributor, coil, points, thermostat, and temperature gauges, everything worked well, and not one flat tire. When they stopped to fix a leak in the radiator on one occasion, Doris the mechanic took charge of plugging the holes with chewing gum. As always, lots of children gathered, and the missionaries had an opportunity to witness to them. One little boy accepted Christ as his Savior. They were reminded again that the Lord ordered their starts and stops. After conference it seemed wise to go by way of Bangui to get some help for the truck. The garage did a good job of changing the necessary parts, and they got back to Bangassou with just one planned stop at Bambari for overnight accommodations.

The drums beat the wake-up call to get everyone going, so they would soon be moving around. Some went to classes; others went to work. About one hundred of their Faithful Women were leaving at 7 a.m. to go door-to-door in town to distribute tracts in stores, in the market, and in homes. Even if the recipients couldn't read, they wanted a tract, and would ask someone else to read its message to them. Doris never saw any that had been torn up or thrown away. As the women came back, they were sad and stated that they had run out of tracts. But at that moment, there were more on the way. Doris had translated them and had them printed in the United States at the cost of $40 for 10,000 tracts.

Doris often said that she would like to be several people so that she could get more of the jobs done. Occasionally, her co-workers of being a "work-horse" accused her. "There is so little time and so much to do." One morning in prayer meeting, one of the ladies said, "Lord, we thank you for all of the extra strength that you give Doris to get all of this work done." Doris reminded the ladies that there were many people back home caring and praying for the spiritual and physical needs of not only the missionaries, but also of the Africans. Although the missionaries weren't in Africa principally to improve physical health conditions, the applied truth of God's message changed not only their hearts, but also the physical and material conditions of the people. As the missionaries would take road trips into the bush, the marked difference jumped out at them as they noted the living conditions of a village that still hadn't heard of Christ's love for them, compared to one where the message of God's love had reached hearts and changed lives. They knew what God could do in lives, and seeing changed lives was a source of constant joy and praise.

Writer, Editor, and Publisher

"Whoopee!" If you had been within hearing distance, you would have heard Doris shout upon the completion of the third set of children's lessons in the Sango language. She had purposed in her heart that the lessons would be done that month. Some of the material could be translated from the English, but some had to be compiled and rewritten according to the culture of the people. Can you imagine preparing lessons on the Tabernacle and the offerings in a way that unschooled (they were not ignorant) people could grasp the spiritual blessings and truths involved? How did she manage that? Prayer warriors and caring Christians in the States were praying. Ruth Bartow took over Doris' children's classes for a month, and Doris would begin work on the Tabernacle lessons each morning at 4 a.m. The first draft had to be sent to a member of the language committee for correction. It was checked for language errors and for anything that could be misinterpreted doctrinally, and then returned to Doris for typing. Next she needed to find a picture or draw one to help the students visualize the truths of each lesson. When this was all done, Doris sent them to the Brethren Mission Press at Bozoum, and prayed that they would not get lost. One set of corrected lessons took two weeks to go 200 miles by registered mail. These lessons were used by Baptist Mid-Missions, Africa Inland Mission, the Swiss Pentecostal Mission, and the Brethren Mission, who also profited from them in their work. She praised God for the praying Christians at home who were concerned and had interceded for the project, too. All this was done without the modern advantages of computers and word processors. All the work was done by hand, or on a manual typewriter.

Faithful Women Testimonies around the Campfire at a Conference

"In the times of my childhood, to see a campfire meant that we were going to give offerings to Gassaroma, a heathen god, and dance around the fire all night to please him. Since the missionaries have come with God's message of salvation, I am no longer under that bondage that my parents knew, because I have Christ as my Savior."

"Praise the Lord, I am His. My parents gave me to Gakola, another god, when I was a baby because they knew only darkness. But now I know Christ and I have peace within my heart. I'm no longer full of fears as were my forefathers."

"Before the missionaries came, we (the women) were like animals. Now we know the way of faith in Christ, and besides that they teach us how to act and live."

"My relatives tied me to a stick for days and then chased me into the woods when I refused to dance for the heathen god, Gassaroma. It is so sad. They didn't know any better for they were in darkness without the message of the real God." Everyone was very tired, but many, many more shared joyful testimonies until they had to close to go rest. It was worth it all, folks.

Conference time for the missionaries meant living in mud huts often accompanied by goats, chickens, dogs, eating African food, making do without conveniences, taking baths in a pail, cracking their heads on doorways (doors were made at bending height), and sleeping on cots or on the ground, trusting that the bugs wouldn't be too plentiful or keep them awake.

One day, Doris received mail that was sent out to the village. She read some of it by flashlight under a mosquito net. One pastor wrote, "We want you to know that we are praying for you. God bless you with strength each day and encouragement of heart and mind as you do battle for Him there in the heart of Africa." Other letters from home assured her of the people's prayers for her. How often her heart had been encouraged by the letters from home, reminding her that she wasn't forgotten at the throne of God's grace. Then too, Doris could hear the ladies in the camp praying for "mademoiselle."

The missionaries taught music, hygiene, and personal soul winning. The Africans were great at memorization. The women came on foot, many as far as seventy-five miles, with babies tied on their backs and their food and clothing in a bundle on their heads. Doris was usually the only teacher, with the classes going from 7.m. until dark. Those women were so eager to come to the conference to learn more from God's Word that the effort in getting there did not seem to kill their desire to come. All of their enthusiasm and efforts were a big help and push for Doris to keep going. By the end of the day she didn't have much strength left, but God promised to "supply all of her needs" (Philippians 4:13). He always keeps His promises.

There were about 1,600 people present at the Easter program. The young people and children quoted 120 verses collectively, and these were interspersed with songs sung in four-part harmony by the young people. The delightful dessert was to see thirty-six people step out to accept Christ as their Savior at the close of the celebration of the resurrection of the Savior.

More Travel

Did you ever travel along a jungle road through grass that bowed over the engine as you burrowed through, with twelve inches of water in the tracks and rain pelting down from the sky? Did you ever have your motor get wet and quit, and as you stick your little piggy's into the water to try to get to the motor to dry it off you hear the back tire gently whisper "pssst" to let you know that it is going flat? Did you ever have a floating jack that didn't want to co-operate, so you only knew success when you crawled under the car into the water with a machete to cut the grass and dig a hole for the jack? Did you ever have a torsion bar arm break, even though a mechanic in the United States said that it never happens? (As a result, it took six hours to go fifty miles). Did you ever go miles and miles into the "unreached areas" and find pastors building churches, having baptism classes, and training children? Or see them stop what they were doing and run towards you calling "mama, mama" because you had helped in their Bible school training before they went to the area of outreach? Or hear them, after the usual greeting, asking questions about the Word of God and the Christian life? And finally, did you ever feel so full of joy for the privilege of ministering for Him that problems with vehicles and physical fatigue seemed minute? If the answer is "yes," you understand completely Doris' heart.

On one occasion, they traveled ten hours through grass taller than themselves, and water so high that they had to think about the wiggly creatures that might be living there. They came to broken bridges that they often needed to be repaired before crossing with the truck, and finally arrived at the village of Madambari. At that time, chief Madambari had many, many wives and thirty-nine children. The missionaries told the chief that they had come to show him, and the people of his village, God's Word and His love for Him. He answered, "I know all of these words, and when God takes away my desire for strong drink and women, I'll believe."

Wherever they went, everyone wanted a tract or some piece of literature. They all paid a small portion for their Bibles and literature, and the missionaries subsidized the rest. Those who couldn't read would ask a school child to read it to them. Even though the missionaries would arrive with oodles of Bibles, books, and scripture portions as they made these trips, there was never enough. Many were the tears of those who were left out.

Four years after the Rebellion's massacre at the time of their independence in the Belgian Congo, Doris and some of the Africans crossed the Mboumou River in a dugout canoe to check on the missionaries' homes and living conditions. It was the first time anyone had gone back. An enormous amount of destruction was still evident. Ransacked houses and abandoned vehicles that had been gutted and completely destroyed were a heart-wrenching sight. Several bullets were found in the tree where they had tied the villagers as prisoners before they were shot. Soldiers were living in the houses that were still habitable. Even though the hearts of Doris' group were very heavy from the sights of destruction and death, they were praising God that He had spared them and their homes in the Central African Republic from the same destiny.

So Busy, How Could They Best Use Their Time and Strength

They often asked themselves, "What have we done or are we doing wrong," as they met together to find solutions to daily accomplish everything that they envisioned getting done for their Lord. Some of the questions needed an answer from Him. They waited on Him to direct concerning these needs: "scheduling time to write more Sunday school lessons. The language committee is now reviewing and correcting the last set that Doris finished. Another set will be needed very soon."

- "Wisdom to know how to fund the production of tracts and other materials as they go to press."

- "Ink, paper, stencils for the mimeograph, run off letters, class materials, etc."

- "Roof for the carport so that the kitchen won't have rain coming in around the door, and to protect the kerosene stove and refrigerator from getting wet."

- "Twenty more student houses need to be built in the near future. Time? Money?"

- "The present refrigerator will go back to Bakouma. Can we afford to replace it?"

What they really needed the most were more *missionaries*! The above needs were minimal in comparison to the financial needs of the missionary families who were waiting to return. The material items would have been a big help in the work, but they were secondary to the need for servants to give out God's Word. But they had much to thank the Lord for as He made their hearts glad in the ministry He had helped them fulfill for His glory.

God's Promises

"Greater is He that is in you than He that is in the world," "power belongeth unto God," "He is my Defense and my Fortress"; these, and many others, were all promises from God's Word that Doris could claim as she prepared to launch out for the Ouango area. As an ambassador for Christ she was heading to share these same truths with hundreds of women who would be attending one of the four Faithful Women's conferences. She would enjoy the fellowship for three to four days in each place, as well as sharing God's Word before journeying on to the next place to minister.

First, she had to get there. Three miles from home the radiator began to boil. As she waited for the motor to cool a bit, she checked the tires and decided that she needed to add a bit of air in them as the load was pretty heavy, and real roads were non-existent. There were rocks, mud holes, and gullies to straddle. If they were too wide, you must gently go down one bank and up the other. The three spare tires she had with her, none of which would pass inspection in the United States, were necessary because changing a tire was part of making the trip an adventure. Rarely did just one spare tire suffice on those roads.

Although extremely fatigued with having meetings all day, God had laid the burden on her heart to encourage and teach these dear ladies God's message from His Word to their hearts. As the villages and areas were so many, Doris could only schedule one conference a year for several churches in the area. Their testimonies and comments helped Doris remember that she was serving a Loving, Almighty God:

"Thank you for coming to us with encouragement from God's Word."

"Please pray for me as I go back to the village. My husband told me that he would cut my throat upon my return if I came to this conference. Since I have arrived here at the conference, he has sent word that he will kill me."

"Five of my family died this year. Pray that I'll know how to obey God's Word and 'Rejoice always' as it tells us to do in Philippians."

"My husband beats me when I refuse to make palm wine for him."

"My husband is possessed of evil spirits and has been in stocks for several months now."

One group of twenty ladies was stopped and threatened by a soldier on their way to the conference because they were not in their gardens. The missionaries had obtained permission from all of the officials, even the chiefs, of the bush areas to hold the conferences. One lady said, "He got his switch and was going to beat us, but God wouldn't let him." Later, the officials reprimanded the soldier. God gave foresight to the missionaries to provide a copy of the official permission from the government authorities for the ladies to carry as they traveled.

They sang, "The joy of the Lord is my strength," with a thankful heart as each conference closed, and journeyed back to the mission station and home. God had allowed her to minister to about 800 women who attended one of the four conferences. God's Word says, "Thy shoes shall be as iron and brass; and as thy days, so shall thy strength be" (Deuteronomy 33:25). She was so weary upon returning to the station, but realized how privileged she was to be called of God to see changed hearts and lives through sharing God's Word with a very needy people.

Tireless in Bangui

When she tried to order two new tires and inner tubes from the capital, Doris was informed that there were none that fit the truck. She asked the ladies to pray about this because "her tires were all "tired out." Thus one woman prayed, "Now God, you know how tired the tires are on her truck. You know too, she has to go over another awful road to another conference. Even though the tires have died, we want you to give them life again."

Surprise! Oh really? Doris got some new tires! Unless you have been on the mission field in like circumstances, this will be hard to believe. The men on the station changed all of the wheels and tires to a different size, from fifteen-inch wheels to sixteen-inch wheels. Why would they do such a thing? It was costly, of course, but our God is a great God. Philippians 4:13 doesn't say a few of our needs, but *all* needs will be supplied. Five complete wheels and tires and one extra tire. The truck from which the wheels were taken belonged to another missionary and had been condemned to the junk yard. Therefore, it didn't need its wheels anymore, and there was still rubber on the tires. Then too, that size tire could be bought in Bangui. Being bigger, they even raised the truck a bit, thus disturbing fewer anthills and rocks in the middle of the roads.

On another occasion, Elizabeth Jewell and Doris went to the Bakouma district for a conference, and their hearts were encouraged. For a distance of ten miles to make the trip easier for them, the believers had cut the grass that was in the middle of the road, and repaired bridges and filled holes so that Miss could find the road to get to Noukoussa. There were twenty-five more miles that the villagers didn't have time enough to clear, but the welcome at the end of the line was tremendous.

That term she was teaching personal evangelism, Bible history, French, and music in the Bible school program, teaching four-part harmony with an accordion. Some of the missionaries who really knew music wondered how she managed that little feat. The quartets surprised them all with their harmony, none more so than their teacher.

There were over one hundred children in class every morning, five days a week. For a change of pace, Doris decided to teach them the game of baseball. They had many laughs attempting to teach baseball for recreation: "If you hit the ball, run!"

"Left or right?"

"Who cares which way we run around the bases?" They didn't throw the ball to their team to get an out. They tried hard to hit the runner instead. I imagine that that was the teacher's fault, don't you? Their teacher had lots of huffs and puffs in the teaching process.

Teenagers came for class in the afternoon when they were not in the gardens, cooking, or taking care of little brothers and sisters.

Preparation for classes, conferences, and writing Sunday school lessons was done as much as possible in daylight. The electric motor was on for a couple of hours in the evening if it was working. Otherwise, they used kerosene lamps and lanterns, and all the bugs and mosquitoes became their guests. Sleeping under a mosquito net was a way of life. If you were careful that the lamp didn't get placed too close to the net, you could read under the net.

Dombima

"Mademoiselle, may I speak with you a little to share the burden on my heart?" Dombina's husband, who now had six other wives, had forbidden her to come to the house of the Lord. Today, he had sent her to the coffee plantation where she had worked for awhile, and then came by way of the garden to the conference. To avoid trouble, Doris asked for three volunteers from the ladies present to go help her pick coffee during their normal free time to eat so that she could come back to the conference in the afternoon. Her husband had told her that if she continued going to the mission, that either the pastor could pay him for the price he had paid for her, or that he would kill her as she was no longer any use to him.

"Miss, you tell me what I should do." "Miss" wasn't wise enough to know how to counsel her, but she knew that God could. If Dombina left her husband, she would forfeit her four children, and someone would have to pay back the money. If she stayed, she would continue to be beaten and abused, and go to an early grave at twenty-eight years of age. She was shaking so much she could hardly hold the cup of coffee that Doris put in her hands. Many of these dear women were living in like conditions. Nevertheless, during the campfire meeting the same evening, Dombina gave one of the sweetest testimonies of God's grace and faithfulness.

A couple of Frenchmen drove by when Doris was at the conference and said, "Do you mean to tell us that you are here all alone?" They meant, of course, "Are you the only white person here?"

Doris answered, "No, I'm not alone as all these women are here with me." There are no anxious moments when all colors and races love the same Lord.

The truck had reason to moan, as love gifts of several pounds of rice, chickens, about fifty eggs, two huge pineapples (fifteen pounds each), and several bags of peanuts were added to the load. These people were so grateful and generous. Many times they had very little food for themselves and their families, but wanted to give the very best to God's messengers. The missionaries learned many lessons from these dear ones.

A Day in the Life of Doris

Doris ran downtown to pick up the weekly mail from the post office. That in itself was excitement for one day, for one and all. Doris said, "Nothing much happens around here." Well, Djiambi had just dug a jigger out of her toe, of course that was a story often repeated. Then too, the student who was a cripple was there busy dissecting Christmas cards. The plain parts went to Ruth to use at the dispensary; the parts with the pictures got a verse stamped on them in the Sango language and were given out as awards for the children. One of Doris' girls who was married with two children, was there learning embroidery to earn money to feed her children; her husband was a student, but hadn't turned out very good. There were two students cutting grass with corn knives fastened to long sticks, Elie was sweeping the dirt off the brick walls, and Pata the dog made the rounds to all with two short yips to say, "Good morning." Pamby the goat followed Pata, jumping and prancing on her hind legs to get Pata to chase her. The mice were chewing suitcases and Tupperware, and the termites were chewing everything that they could find. A big black cobra had killed two mother hens and swallowed the chicks. Those were the last chicks that it would ever swallow, as Doris fixed it as a specialty dish to serve to one and all on the station. None of the missionaries but Doris had eaten snake meat before.

To finish that dull day, Ruth sent word from the dispensary that the daughter of one of the students had fallen and needed stitches on her head. Doris took her to the hospital at the post to be sewed up. In the afternoon, a missionary woman from the Congo needed to get across the river. She had decided not to take the conventional way of checking with the offices at Bangassou. She wanted to go to the Ouango area where there was no ferry and convince someone to help her cross in a dugout canoe, so they took her as far as they could. She didn't come back, so hopefully that worked, as her visa was to run out the next day. Like Doris said, "It was a dull day." They did find a few things to kill time, so that they didn't get homesick.

A Happy Chief

"Merci Nzagui, merci Nzagui" (thank God), were the only words that the old chief at Poumbolo could utter the day the missionaries took Pastor Boguini back to his village. In June, he had been bitten by a viper and was taken to the government dispensary at Kembe because his station was closer to Kembe than it was to Bangassou. He wasn't treated there at Kembe because there were little or no medications. Edie Wotherspoon, the Baptist Mid-Missions nurse stationed at Kembe, heard about Boguini and rushed the eight miles to get him and take him to the mission station. By this time he was close to death. A long, hard struggle followed.

Although he still couldn't walk, in July he was taken to Bangassou, partly on a bike and the rest of the way in a car so that he could give lectures in teaching truths from the Old Testament for two weeks. It appeared that he might lose his foot, but after several weeks the big hole produced from the snake venom began to heal. Dr. Fisher from the mission hospital at Ippy, took a trip by a Missionary Aviation Fellowship plane to Bangassou to do a skin graft to help it heal. It was then decided that he could go home, although it wasn't yet healed completely. Upon his arrival back in his village, the chief Poumbolo couldn't believe that Pastor Boguini was well. After his ecstatic greeting to Yango, he said, "Thanks to you missionaries we have our pastor back. You patiently cared for him all of these months." The missionaries all knew that the praise should go to God alone.

On returning to Bangassou, one of the old deacons at Gambo asked Doris to take some things to Bangassou. The truck was already heavily loaded, and with the roads being so bad she had to tell him "no." He said, "You are wicked." After musing a bit he brought her two big handfuls of bananas.

She said, "Do you want to give a gift to a wicked person?" and he replied,

"Oh, mademoiselle, you aren't wicked." She deduced that it was a peace offering.

A Visit from Ruth Nephew

It was nice to have Ruth Nephew back "home" for a three-week visit during January when classes were closed for the gardening. As usual, Doris and Ruth found so much humor in daily events, thus making her visit a reunion of joy for Doris even when strength seemed to be lacking. Naturally, Ruth's visit called for another outstation trip. Traveling towards their destination, only thirteen miles away this time, they came upon a little old lady standing, with her stick for support, in the middle of the road. When the girls stopped to check, they found that she couldn't walk, but only shuffle. They told her to wait in the shade beside the road, and they would pick her up after the services on down the road.

After the service, upon inquiring about the pastor's oldest daughter, they were told that she was sick. After seeing her at home and checking on her physical needs, Doris sent for the two Ruths, both nurses who had made the trip with her, to come and see her. The decision was made to bring her back to the station with them. Not yet even in her teens, she already had the reputation of being a harlot. When asked about her spiritual health, even though she had heard the gospel many times, her reply was, "I don't really know." They returned home with two patients needing help physically, but most of all they were concerned about their spiritual and thus, eternal needs.

Soul Winning

Missionaries see many physical and material needs, but God had called them and placed them there for a much more vital ministry. As Paul said in Acts 26:18, "To open their eyes, and to turn them from darkness to light, and from the power of Satan unto God, that they may receive forgiveness of sins, and inheritance among them which are sanctified by faith that is in me." The Faithful Women, as they did a canvass of every house in Bangassou, were aware that the best cure with eternal benefits was to share God's message with others that someone had shared with them. Although many of the people who received the tracts didn't know how to read, they gladly received them because they knew that they could find someone to read it to them.

One Saturday afternoon, the ladies all went out soul winning. Some of them went as far as eight miles away from the conference on foot. When they returned, the missionaries counted the little twigs that they had brought back with them. Each twig represented a decision made to follow Christ. In less than six hours time of sharing the gospel, there were forty twigs on the pile representing souls saved, and forty-nine twigs on the pile representing those that prayed to get their lives right in God's sight. Remember these were ladies who didn't know how to read, write, or calculate. Their money was counted in fives, thus they did their piles by counting by fives. Doris asked them, "Did you pray for me and the conference in Ouango?"

The answer came loud and clear, "Is there any day that we forget to pray for you, our Mademoiselle?"

One of the ladies who was doing distribution had a strangulated hernia, but they waited twenty-four hours before sending a runner to tell Doris. When Doris took her to the hospital, the nurse on guard was drunk, and it took a great deal of time and energy before he understood that the surgeon was needed right away. A drunken anesthesiologist arrived, but still no surgeon. Before the surgeon finally arrived, the woman's condition had worsened. Hopeless? No. God is God; He is the Great Physician, and she did survive.

Ruth had worked and prayed over a five month old baby who had a very high temperature and convulsions. When they took the baby to the French doctor at the post, he told Ruth that she had done all she could. They kept the baby at the hospital, but as the nurse on duty was drunk, he received little or no care, and died.

The Association Meeting of the Baptist Churches

The Baptist Mid-Missions missionaries and the African pastors of the churches had met together a few times over the course of time to try to encourage and help each other in their ministries. Satan doesn't like for Christians to have good fellowship and harmony in the gospel, thus he started some division among the brethren. All reports of the association meetings had been very positive until a few of the pastors from the Ouango area had heard that the World Council of Churches would send them money if they would leave the Baptists and accept a missionary from their organization. Since there was no resident missionary in the Ouango area at the time, the men from the Bangassou area added Ouango to their already full program. Bob Golike called a meeting with all the pastors in the area to iron out the misunderstandings. Most of their dear pastors were real servants of the Lord with a burden for souls. However, there was just a few that wanted the financial promises of the World Council. This continued to cause heartache for the missionaries and African pastors who carried the burden of seeking the lost for Christ. The few rebels said that the missionaries neglected them.

Doris already had four Faithful Women's conferences in their area scheduled for the month of June during Bible school vacation. There just weren't any available missionaries to send to reside in their area. As it was, Bangassou station, where the Bible school was located didn't have enough missionaries to adequately staff the work there. However, Bob and Marilea Golike needed to move to the capital, Bangui, to take care of urgent needs there. The ladies on the station needed to hold the fort by themselves until the Chasteens arrived in a couple of months.

Ruth had her hands full with about two hundred people to treat each morning, five days a week. Sometimes she was busy at the dispensary until she needed to go to one of her afternoon classes. The girls needed much wisdom and strength from the Lord. Doris continually praised God for the great cloud of witnesses around the world that did not cease to pray for them. Dependability, after the need to be saved, had been drilled into the minds of the Gilbert kids. Remember, Doris went to school for twelve years without missing a day. It wasn't her idea, but it was good formation! Doris knew that God would enable her to do things that she never expected to be called on to do for the Lord, and thus mankind.

One day in June, Ruth sent a runner to the classroom, "Miss, you must go to the dispensary at once. There is a lady that is demon-possessed, and Mademoiselle Doctor said that you would know how to pray with her and talk with her until she would ask for deliverance by the power of God." After praying and sharing the Scripture with her for a couple of hours, Doris saw victory as the lady trusted Christ as her Savior. The battle against the principalities and powers can leave one so weak. Leaning on the everlasting arms for every ounce of wisdom and strength needed, Doris knew that she must believe in the power of God more than she ever had before. How precious it was to know and experience the truth of God's power. Phil 4:13 says, "I can do all things through Christ who strengthens me." God said it—I believe it.

On a trip to an outstation, not too much happened—well, besides that they didn't have any brakes for eighty miles and needed to change a broken shock. They couldn't take care of those things until they got back to the station where there was a pit. Incidents like this had become so common, about as compared to running out of gas when traveling in the United States; maybe a little different, since so much is the "do-it yourself" system in Africa.

Baptism Class

With over one hundred people lined up waiting to meet the deacons and missionaries to share personal testimonies of their salvation experience, questions were echoing across the building such as, "Why do you want to be baptized?" This was to encourage each one to tell of their personal acceptance of Christ as their Savior.

Some would reply, "Jesus was baptized, wasn't He?" The hearts of the missionaries were always glad to see that these dear people wanted to be identified with Christ by being baptized. Some of the questions that were asked of the candidates for baptism included,

"Do you know how to read?" There were daily reading classes to help them to be able to at least read some verses from the Bible that gave them assurance of God's work in their lives.

"Do you beat your wife?" No.

Or maybe they answer among other things, "Only when she refuses to go to bed with me."

"Are you a complaining wife?"

"Are you a man or woman of two tongues (two-faced)?"

"How many wives do you have?" If a plural number of wives was the answer, they were not to be baptized until they have taken care of their marital situation. Dowries could be costly, and the woman's family wasn't too eager to return the money or other payments, such as goats, chickens, cows, food, or money that they had received when they sold their daughters or sisters.

After all were questioned, if their answers showed that they are born-again and living Christ-honoring lives, their names were added to the list of those to be baptized. The missionary men always looked for an area where the river was cleaner to have the baptism services. "Next" was the cry from the deacons and missionaries who were waiting in the river to baptize one after another.

Does this sound like a complicated process? God's servants prayed much that they would have wisdom. Mob psychology was prevalent, thus the cry went up to God for discernment to know how to build a solid ministry that was God-honoring and would last. Not many years previously, this land had been completely controlled by Satan worship; therefore, there was a continuous battle to keep God's work untouched by some of the hideous practices of darkness. Naturally, as God's work grew and honored Him, Satan, the author of sin and darkness, used his wiles to try to destroy it. He tempted some of the pastors, deacons and leaders with worldly pride and the desire to be like some of the chiefs of old who had sought complete devotion and servitude from the people. They especially expected the African women who had become Christians to serve them.

Doris continued to be very busy with the regular daily programs on the station. The joy of the conferences for the Faithful Women continued to delight her heart and soul. By August, she had included seven conferences in her schedule in the outstations, with exciting results for the Lord. A total of 1,317 women had come to be taught and enriched by God's Word. Through their door-to-door evangelism in the villages, which was always part of conference program, 968 people accepted Christ as Savior, and 603 came back to the Lord. Their precious time together, learning how to live "God's way" was very enriching. They were together exclaiming that they enjoyed the godly language and could converse together without any backbiting or dirty words like they got at home.

Some of the questions sought godly direction about their marital situations and home life: "My husband is a Christian; why does he continue to beat me?" This was a question even asked by some pastors' and deacons' wives.

"Do I have to sleep with my husband the same day the baby is born?" To Doris, the old-maid missionary, some of the subjects were quite shocking. However, she always took some godly African ladies with her to the conferences who could give good counsel and direction for these dear ones who had experienced little, if ever any, respect from the time they were born.

The question, voiced by many of the ladies that shocked Doris the most was, "How many months do we need to work in the pastor's garden or coffee plantation before we can be baptized?" Doris didn't have an answer to that very delicate situation. She hadn't graduated with a degree in psychology, nor did she know how to give a satisfying answer that would be acceptable to both the pastors and the women.

"Pass the buck" seemed to be the wisest move to make. She told them that she would share that question with the men when she returned to the mission station. Slavery had been very much a way of life within the culture. She didn't approve of anything that made life harder for her ladies. It was evident that African culture, much of which is good, played a big role in this subject.

Wow! Did that ever bring out issues that no one expected! Doris soon learned that it was not unusual. The next step after accepting Christ as their Savior was to prepare for baptism. Surprisingly enough, most of the pastors considered that having "volunteers" to work in their gardens was normal. What an unbelievable surprise and heartache this was to all of the missionaries. Where had they failed in sharing the message that salvation was by grace alone, no works or money needed? Salvation is free because Christ loved us and died for our sins.

She loved her ladies, but it didn't stop there. Children's classes five days a week kept her excited as the children grew in knowledge of God's Word and His will for their lives. There were laughs by the bushels as the oldest to the youngest came up with amusing and new ideas for learning and playing. One kid comically decided to make a hat out of the skin of a grapefruit. It worked, too. They delighted in making her laugh. One day the girls decided that they wanted to braid "Mademoiselle's" hair the African way. Comments included, "Her hair isn't obedient. As soon as I braid a lock, it bounces back out. Her hair is weak and doesn't stand up like ours. When I start on the second braid the first one falls out." They could make all kinds of designs with their own hair by blocking it off into sections and then winding each lock with black thread. Their hair just stayed that way. As they giggled and worked they finally decided to close the beauty shop as their client was a lost cause.

Although their classes included singing, learning to read and write, cleanliness and health, her greatest delight was teaching memorization of the Scriptures. They could and would learn whole chapters from God's Word. One little four-year old named Gilberte learned and recited twenty-seven verses for the Easter program. All of the little tykes recited Psalm 23.

Many of the children didn't have the choice of going to government schools, as the schools were so few and far away. Many children were sent to relatives who lived near where the schools existed, but at least eighty percent didn't have that possibility until they were older, if at all. This is no longer the case, as many of the Africans have excelled in their studies as they have had opportunities to learn. Unlearned does not mean deficient; as their opportunities to learn increased, so did their skills. Multiple are the ones that top their classes as they go on to higher education in the universities in other countries.

The children knew that Doris really loved them. They would clap their hands and dance around as they saw her coming down the lane to the children's chapel. The love was mutual, and they knew it. Oh, the happy faces of children as Doris gave them the gifts that ladies' groups in the United States had made for them, such as cute little headscarves for the girls, who all wore something on their heads. Children's clothes for all ages were collected and packed in the barrels to share with the children in Africa when Doris went back after furlough. One and all got a real kick, as they strutted and showed off their new finery. It was worth all the effort in getting the clothes together, packing them in barrels, listing item by item, and shipping them to Africa. As a rule, no taxes were charged. Normally, she had about one hundred kids each morning. She needed a good plan to distribute the clothing justly. Everyone received something, but memorization of Scriptures qualified some for an additional garment or gift.

Part of the schedule was to check hands and faces to see if they were clean. There was water at the chapel for those who "forgot."

Doris and her helpers discovered that the children's new clothes were not being washed. Day by day, Doris and her helpers told them to go to the river and wash their clothes before the next day rolled around. After several days of warnings, nothing changed. The children came with dirty clothes the next day. They were sent to get some big leaves to wear to cover the dirt. They thought that it was funny, and no one washed their clothes. Kids aren't too different around the world, and they brought the leaves to put on a show. When Doris said that she would take a picture, the kids became excited about having their picture taken so they could see how they looked dressed in leaves. Instead of this becoming an act of discipline, the idea backfired. Everyone was getting a big chuckle out of the whole procedure, the children and the teachers included.

This was the start of one of the darkest moments of Doris' life. The rebels carried the news to the local officials that Doris was making fun of the children, and that she should be sent out of the country. Needless to say, Doris was very shocked and humbled by all of these doings. The work of the Lord was encouraging to her and the others. It was thrilling to experience God's special blessing and working in the hearts of their people. Not only were their hearts blessed to see God's work among the children, many enthusiastic and dedicated soul winners developed among the women as they became more and more aware of the worth of each soul to which they ministered.

The women were enthused about their special conferences. Then too, the increased support from the local authorities was an unexpected and delightful addition to their joy. As local government authorities came out to the mission to check up on Doris, even those who loved and appreciated her and her Lord didn't dare deny the accusations against her. After all, they were just women, and their opinion wasn't worth considering, even if they had dared to say anything. The local government authorities were aware that there had been a recent government notice stating that there was perfect liberty to take pictures in the Central African Republic. Probably, in a quandary as to the next step to take, showing their authority, the decision was made to send her to the higher authorities at Bangui, the capital.

Doris and Dean Chasteen, the missionary who was the head of the station at that time, received word that they were "invited" to meet with one of the national government officials in Bangui. Upon arriving in Bangui, five hundred miles from Bangassou, Doris was put under house arrest for about three weeks awaiting the call to come before the judge.

The believer's steps are ordered of the Lord. These are not experiences that we would choose, but God is in control, and surely there are lots of lessons to be learned. Doris especially was trying to constantly apply the verse, "Yea, though I walk through the valley of death, I will fear no evil: for Thou art with me; Thy rod and Thy staff they comfort me." This was applicable to agonies of the spirit in the midst of her life. Doris prayed, "Lord, make me a testimony of Your grace and peace in this time of being pressed and oppressed." May the hidden gold that the Lord has laid up for us be revealed during these days. When we are satisfied with His will and way, there is rest. She didn't always apply these truths to her heart and life, but being totally in the school of God she knew that day by day and with each passing moment she was in the care of Almighty God.

Finally, one of the missionaries who assumed that she should have been more agitated came to ask her, almost scoldingly, if she realized what a mess she was in. Her answer, "I try to be completely resting in the everlasting arms of my God." Yes, she had some sleepless nights and wondered what the future held for her, but she tried to continually remember that He held the future.

One of her faithful women leaders came all the five hundred miles from Bangassou to Bangui to cheer her and to bring greetings from others. She threw her arms around Doris as she sobbingly said, "Many, many hundreds of people are praying for you. We love you so very much." They had a prayer meeting together. Doris thanked God for these dear ones praying at Bangassou; it was like medicine for her heart to have precious and loving moments together with one of these dear ones.

From time to time Doris was called in to meet someone in authority during her house arrest who would give the official decision on the case. She kept getting messages from the people at Bangassou such as "Miss, don't get discouraged, we will pray you back here."

"We really, really love you, please don't abandon us."

"The children's classes are empty without you here. The children ask for you every day." She shares this to underline the greatness of our God and the power of prayer. There were lots of good servants of the Lord that remained at Bangassou, but all this did encourage her heart so much.

Finally, Doris was told that the vice-president of the country would be meeting with her the next day. Wow! What's next! He graciously offered her a seat and immediately stated, "All of these accusations are ridiculous." He began to tell her about the people in the tribe from which he came. "The men especially are very jealous of each other, and it appears that it is a hateful jealousy of one man who has encouraged all of these allegations that are upon you. I do fear for your life as this man wants to kill you."

He told Doris the man's name, which was no surprise to her. She and the women had had many prayer meetings for him. He was an intelligent fellow, and when devoted to the Lord, he could do great things for God. They had a friendly conversation as he congratulated her on her devotion to the women of the country. Before she left his office, as she was due for furlough in a few months, he gave her the visa to return to the Central African Republic after her furlough. As a reminder of how God takes care of His own, she has kept this visa all of these years. Although her camera had been confiscated at Bangassou, she had the film and made a copy of the picture that Satan used to cause all of the upheaval. God never makes mistakes. Doris knows that He had lots of lessons to teach her through this trial, the magnitude of which she couldn't yet know.

Upon returning, after the long journey back, the road into the mission station was lined with people waving flowers, clapping their hands, and yelling, "You did come, you did come," from the beginning of the mission road until her house. They knew that Doris was supposed to arrive sometime that day, and had been there waiting all day long. They hugged her, and some reached through the crowd surrounding her and rubbed her arms when they couldn't get close. The women screamed and hugged Doris, the children clapped, and they all rejoiced: "We haven't been able to sleep or eat properly since you have been going through all of this trouble."

"We prayed even while we hoed our gardens."

"God only know the tears we have shed as we prayed and wept for your deliverance."

"Do some men think that they can make walls of water in the river? God is bigger than man. Some men just think they are important."

"Miss, don't let your spirit break because of a few. There are many, many of us that love you and want you here with us."

It would require several chapters to mention all of the comments. Many fasted and prayed for days. God rewarded their faith, and they were all together having a big time of thanksgiving. Sometimes the road was pretty rough, but she learned from those experiences and continued to praise the dear Lord.

Doris was beat and needed her scheduled furlough. However, Bible school graduation services and the transportation of the graduates and their families back home was on the program, followed by the Baptist Mid-Missions field conference five hundred miles each way. Since this was so soon after the special trials He had allowed Doris to go through, many caring co-workers assured her of their prayers. However, some do have funny ways of sympathizing and carrying their co-worker's burdens. Those who know her well knew that Doris had a natural tendency to see the glass half full, not half empty. Almost gloatingly, one missionary said, "Now you know that not everyone loves you." Ouch! That hurt, but it was a reminder to ask God to continually help her to use her tongue to edify and continually encourage God's family and the ones they had come to seek and see saved. No, not perfect yet, but He is in the business of perfecting, if we let Him. Psalm 19:14 says, "Let the words of my mouth and the meditation of my heart be acceptable in Thy sight, O, Lord my strength, and my Redeemer."

She started the women's conferences again. There were four scheduled in the Ouango area, and the women prayed, "God, You know that our conferences are like food and water to us poor people in a barren land." Six hundred sixty-nine women were able to leave their gardens and come to the three or four day meetings together. In sharing the gospel message as they did door-to-door evangelization, there were 408 who accepted the message of God's love to their hearts and lives.

A tire was in shreds within five miles of home, but that was their only major problem on their way back to the mission station. Doris changed the tire, and they journeyed on. Her truck groaned under the weight of lots of corn and peanuts, a man with a strangulated hernia, two goats, two chickens, two sick children, a pastor, and another pastor's wife who was going to get medicine for her sick husband. The gas in the tank didn't add much weight. The gauge said that the tank was empty, but she was able to get the sick man to the hospital before she had to siphon gas from the barrel on the back into the truck's gas tank.

While reading in Exodus, at a time when she wondered how she could keep up with all the demands of the schedule, God reminded Doris of the words of wisdom from Exodus 18 given to Moses by Jethro, his father-in-law. He had been trying to do so much all by himself, and he needed to delegate some of the jobs to others. Many of the local leaders of the Faithful Women's group had accompanied Doris to help in the conferences out at the bush stations. Why not have meetings to train leaders to care for some of the work? Many faithful women were already teaching and leading in many capacities, such as children's classes, women's Bible studies, and teenage girl's classes at the local churches around the different areas where their people were giving out the gospel. They sincerely loved to seek for souls, and they could reach their own people better than Doris could.

Another Area and District Seeking Help

Doris had received an invitation from Bambari to come and hold meetings to train leaders for the women there. The decision was made to turn this into a leader's training conference. Many ladies from the outstations were excited about being trained as leaders so that they could help others live lives that honored God. This turned out to be an excellent method for the missionaries to work themselves out of a job, which was exactly the whole purpose of sharing the message of the gospel—multiply to multiply. God had given her the charge, although she didn't know how. But she knew that He had; providing it was all for His glory, her heart would be blessed as she watched Him work in lives once again.

Among her gifts, she discovered that trucking was much in demand. One of the teenage boys needed help to get his palm branches from the jungle to the location where he was building his house. He had been such a faithful, helpful young man and was planning on taking a wife soon. How could she say "no"? Then too, these jungle trucking trips always turned out to furnish lots of laughs and education.

They patiently explained to her how the branches would be tied on with rubber ties strips cut from old inner tubes that they had been collecting. She could add to her book of African wisdom when she learned that hundreds of sandals were made with soles cut from old tires. Due to the condition of the roads, the tires didn't last long on the truck for their original purpose. It turned out that there would still be enough rubber left to travel lots of miles on people's feet.

As Doris and some Africans were traveling along one day going to an outstation, they came upon a tree blocking the road that had been uprooted by elephants. Doris always carried a big machete in the truck for such occasions, but you guessed it. This time it wasn't in the truck. The only sharp tool that they had with them was a penknife. As they pecked away at the tree with the little knife, the elephants were standing around watching to make sure that they did a good job. Doris didn't see the elephants, but she was told about it later. The Africans who were with her didn't tell her that part because they thought she might panic if she saw the elephants standing there. Naturally, it took a couple of hours to cut one limb enough so they could break it off the trunk of the tree. Later, as Doris was reminiscing about the incident, her heart was heavy as she thought of how badly they needed help to get the gospel spread to this needy people. They were pecking away as their strength permitted; nevertheless, so many around them were going to a Christless eternity: "So little time, and so much to do." In retrospect, she knows that they only keep going day and night in the strength of the Lord and by God's grace alone. One dear African lady had knelt as the communion was being served at the church, when the pastor said, "Has anyone been omitted?"

A vision came to her of multitudes of people rising up and crying, "Yes, we have been left out. No one has come to us with the message of God's love for us."

Doris' mother and father celebrated their fiftieth anniversary in December, 1959. In June of the following year, she received a cablegram with the news that her mother had gone home to glory. At the time Doris was very sick in bed with malaria, filaria, and all that goes with it. She was pretty weak, run down, and away from her station when the message came. In fact, one doctor said, "If you were a horse, I'd shoot you because you are so far gone." She was hoping that he was joking.

Doris' Daughter Djiambi

Did you know that Doris had an adopted daughter? She can't tell you all of the story, it would be too long. Djiambi's father came to Doris one day and asked her to take Djiambi as her child. He said that he didn't want Djiambi to grow up in the village because there was too much wickedness there. Back then, the missionaries had enemies of course, and after praying and asking counsel from both whites and blacks, the solution they came up with was that Djiambi would come to live with Doris as her daughter, but also as paid hired help. From the time she moved in as a teenager until she married, she received legal wages. Although there was nothing in writing, the family and everyone else, from that time on, considered her as Doris' daughter. The legal representative for the government was aware of this arrangement, a necessary precaution.

So this very sweet, young lady came to live with Doris. She taught Djiambi to sew, embroider, and write, plus how to cook and bake. They would often read the Word and pray together. The advantage for Doris was that both she and Djiambi's family were comfortable and happy with the solution. She would often go to see her parents in the afternoon and they were grateful that God had led them in this way. Djiambi's brother, Mekpe, was one of the boys that Doris taught how to make pictures from butterfly wings.

Djiambi, was looking through an old Montgomery Ward catalog one evening. After laying it aside she said, "The only thing in the whole catalog that I could enjoy wearing is a blond wig." Djiambi had a good sense of humor. The style in Africa was the wrap-around skirts that come to the ankles. When she compared the skirts displayed in the catalog with their normal clothing, she wasn't impressed with the short skirts pictured in the white man's book.

Later, when a pastor named Kima went to the father to ask to marry Djiambi, he was told that he would need to ask Doris, as she was her mother and father now. Doris told them that Djiambi would be the one to choose, and she did. After she was married, Djiambi and Kima had five children, and they named their oldest daughter Doris Gilbert Kima.

Dispensary and Hospital on Their Station

Every few months, the mission doctor would fly in for a day or so to take care of the critical cases. One lady with a huge double goiter was among those waiting for his arrival. (See pictures). The immense growths just hung heavy from her neck down. She and her husband had come to the dispensary, not because of the goiter but for their six-month-old baby who was diagnosed with anemia. Upon questioning them about the goiter, which had been growing for years, it was revealed that they didn't consider it serious. This was the first time anyone from the medical field had seen her condition. It was sad that they hadn't seen her earlier, as it was too dangerous to try and operate by then.

Many surgeries were done on the sick patients who the nurse had lined up for the doctor's next visit. The usual daily schedule at the dispensary varied quite drastically when the doctors dropped by to help the nurses to do consultations and surgeries. There were always surgeries on the agenda. Yes, sometimes the schedules were so full that they were accompanied by panic. "So little time and so much to do" was apparent as they looked to the Lord for the wisdom and compassion needed to care for these suffering ones.

Every day was prefaced by a challenge from God's Word. "Why take time to preach at them when their bodies needed help?" you might ask. God's Word has an immediate, lasting solution for their eternal needs. Many of these dear ones were in this poor physical condition because of living in sin, for which only God could freely give the cure. The missionaries, themselves blood-bought sinners, didn't forget that they were in that land principally to, "Open their eyes and turn them from darkness to light and from the power of Satan unto God," (Acts 26:18). Spiritual healing is eternal, but the medical crew did a great job of caring for the physical needs as well. More important, God had called them to leave behind a practice with much earthly gain to prepare these needy people for eternity. "Christ died for you because He loves you and offers you eternal life" was not a message that had previously been shared to sin-sick millions in dark Africa.

Weddings & Marriages

More and more, as the Africans came to Christ, they were willing to know God's ways for their lives. Before God's servants came to their country with God's guidebook, the Bible, a little girl could easily be bought and sold to any man, old or young. Naturally, an older man had more cows, goats, and material things than a younger man. Thus he often bought his next bride when she was very young.

She would then go to her future husband's home to learn the ways of his household, and be trained by his mother to be a good wife. He would take her as a real wife as young as nine years old. A child bride became a child mother. Since females had little to say about their own bodies and ways of living, they automatically were slaves to their husbands.

Obviously, there were many things about the practice that caused heartaches and sadness to the missionaries, like many other practices that were not in accord with God's Word. They needed to pray much as they sought the best way to help them. They needed direction to know how to help the African leadership cease to consider the wives and girls as their slaves. Respect and submission is one thing, but cruelty is not godly. Little by little, the African Christians become more and more enlightened.

When Doris was home on furlough she sought out formal dresses that could be used as wedding gowns. Lovely formal dresses came from all over. Some provisions came from her nephew who had a florist shop, where local bridal stores displayed special attire in the show windows of his establishment. Many of these dresses were later given to her to take to Africa. Not that having a wedding dress made the wedding godlier, but it helped to make this a special time for the ladies in the transition from a status of slavery to equality. She had lots of fun dressing many brides, many of whom did not have shoes.

There were no jewelers in the center of Africa, even if they had the funds to buy anything. So a plea for wedding rings was added to her needs as she traveled from church to church in reporting of their ministry. At that time even the dollar stores in the United States had wedding rings; even though they weren't made of gold they represented the vows exchanged by the couple. She made up the wedding veils out of mosquito netting, picked some roses from her bushes, and the ceremony was ready to begin.

They knew the missionaries cared enough to help them follow counsel from God's Word concerning marriage. Naturally, special attention for the bride helped increase the respect from the husband. They kept learning that respect and love for God's Word made for all concerned, peaceful, happy people.

Preparation for the National Evangelistic Campaign

Doris' living and dining room had turned into a classroom for about thirty pastors that would be coming to prepare for the National Evangelistic Campaign. These were key men, well grounded in the Word of God who knew the people and their customs. They would be going to Kembe, Bakouma, Ouango, and all of the outstations of Bangassou. They, in turn, would later gather the people together to share the methods that they had learned about how to lovingly share the gospel message to a lost people. The aim and desire was to reach every home in the Central African Republic with the good news of the gospel.

Doris had prepared and written the program for the Easter play that the kids would produce. This time it was entitled, "Who Will Roll Away the Stone?" She liked the theme of the song, "Spirit, of the Living God, Fall Fresh on Us," so she translated that into Sango to be used in the program. The children were very good at memorization and producing plays. Among other things, Doris was in the process of writing a book of plays that could be used throughout the country. The progress was slowed a bit due to other demands on her time. She had recently written a Bible geography textbook for the Bible school curriculum, which took about one hundred hours to complete.

Another Day with Doris

Did you ever have a tooth out in your kitchen? Since the Paulsons had come from Kembe to Bangassou for the day, the makeshift dental office was set up in Doris' kitchen. Irene proved that you don't have to have an enormous amount of equipment to extract the root of a tooth from Doris' mouth. The Paulsons and Ortons, and possibly some others as well, completed a speed course in dentistry that had been offered to missionaries. Both couples used their training to help missionaries and Africans far and near. Naturally, they didn't use all of the knowledge that they had acquired due to the lack of facilities and equipment. The lack of electricity in many of the places made it impossible for them to use some of their equipment.

Did You Ever?

Did you ever stop to eat by the river and have an audience of at least thirty people watch you eat?

Did you ever see someone hold the telephone receiver upside down and wonder why no one could hear him or her talk? Not guilty! Doris was in a store and had quite a chuckle watching this process. They got angry when she tried to help.

Did you ever find a snakeskin in your bed? Let's look on the bright side: it was just a skin, not a snake.

Did you ever boil seventy-two gallons of drinking water in one week? The hot weather made heavy drinkers out of people. At least it was only water.

Did you ever try having a houseful of people without a fridge? The other residents on the station were great about keeping butter and making ice for her in their refrigerators.

Have you ever lived on the border of another country, where the tourists who are making their trek across the continent are coming and going continually? It wasn't always easy to be gracious, as many tourists took it for granted that the missionaries and mission stations were uniquely for tourists.

The following is a poem that Doris wrote in a prayer letter:

"What have I accomplished here today?
A heart made warm by a cheery smile,
or did I sadden a life with scorn?

What have I accomplished as I
speak a language that's foreign?
Have I clearly shown with life and deeds
what my lips have not yet learned?

Have I accomplished your purpose Lord,
in these days and hours and minutes?
Or has my life been shallow and spent for naught,
nothing worthy in it?

Help me to accomplish Lord,
what you have sent me here to do for you
To love, to give and to live Lord,
with eternity's values in view."

COMMUNICATIONS

Due to computer problems in the home office, the missionaries were having some major problems concerning the gifts and givers. They normally received a monthly statement, even if it took two to three weeks to come. The missionaries were reminded that God's computer never fails, and He has promised to supply every need. It is not that the humans are not trustworthy, however, but that the famous equipment made by man doesn't always co-operate. The communication problem was one of the hardest problems they had to face. Receiving news from loved ones, as well as official business, sometimes only twice a month, was one of the highlights of their lives. For instance, Doris received the cablegram telling of the death of her mother two weeks after it was sent.

ON THE ROAD AGAIN

The following is an excerpt from one of Doris' prayer letters of 1960 entitled, "Shall we go anyway?":

"I don't know, what do you think?" And so went the ambiguous conversation after a heavy rain all night and all morning before the proposed trip to Zime, a rarely traveled road in rainy season.

"Well, we said that we would try, so maybe we'd better."

Ruth Bartow and I started out about 1 p.m., and as we stopped to greet the pastors along the way they said, "You're not going to Zime after a downpour like that?"

"I promised to try and I'm trying." The scenery consisted of water under foot and grass overhead. We progressed quite well until we were five miles from Zime and then, as we started up a steep rocky hill with insufficient momentum, the truck stalled. As is usually the case, there was a small bridge behind us at the foot of the hill. No, I didn't back off from this sluice-type bridge, but its covering was mud and there is where my back wheel decided to sit there for awhile. For nearly three hours, we played in the mud. As we tried to jack up the wheel, the jack sunk but the truck didn't rise a bit. Did you ever try to jack up a back wheel on a '61 Chevy truck? You begin by doing a crawl on your paunch to get to where you can get a jack under the rear axle. Don't forget to take a machete with you to clear a place for the jack to stand upright. Anyway, that's the way I proceed because if there is a simpler way, I haven't been notified. The more we jacked, the more we burrowed, progressively producing a playground for woodchucks.

In this country even along the most isolated road, one is not alone for long. People began to gather and joined in the mud game, but the only thing that developed was our muscles. A little after five o'clock the folks from Zime began to come. There must have been about two hundred. Little and big, including several of the Pioneer girls who weren't big enough to help, but they had to see 'Miss' in the mud. After tying a long hemp rope to the front bumper, about thirty-five people latched on to that and others started pushing. Thus, we perambulated for about two kilometers (about 1½ miles) ascending a worn, slippery hill. Due to the density of the population, my visibility was zero, so I just trusted that I wasn't being led astray. We locomoted independently for a short way, but for the grand finale, in the dark, we had to be pushed and pulled up the grass-covered hill road to the mission. After removing our mud packs, which didn't help my complexion much, and the girls had run back the five miles from where the truck was stuck, we had a real nice campfire service with over one hundred girls and their leaders.

On Sunday, we met with the people for services and then started our journey back. We didn't get stuck in the mud this time, but the same back wheel decided that it wanted to rest awhile between two logs in a bridge. Since it was noon, I told the rest that I had the best place as I crawled once again under the shade of the truck to jack up the rear axle. With the help of my two jacks and two inch boards which I always carry with me, in about an hour we were on our way again. Lying on the bridge was much cleaner than lying in the mud. I think four-wheel drive would be advantageous on a vehicle at times."

All is Not a Bed of Roses Unless You Major on the Thorns

In many of the churches in the Central African Republic, exploitation of the members was often practiced by the church officials. Paying or working for the privilege of being baptized, taxing of church members, paying for communion and so forth. The missionaries had become increasingly alarmed. At their field conference, the missionaries were of one mind that these practices were not Biblical. The missionary men had tried to teach the pastors that these practices were not honoring to God, and many of the pastors wanted to do things God's way. They often had to take more abuse from the remaining few who wanted to continue to make their members pay them in one way or another.

Doris had discovered this practice when she was asked about it at a Faithful Women's conference. Lande was the pastor at the mission station, and his attitude had become quite anti-missionary. He wasn't especially happy that Doris had found out some of these practices at that conference. When Doris asked some of the people why he turned on her especially, their answer was, "He is jealous."

To the question, "Jealous of what?" they answered, "He is jealous of the love and devotion that the people have for you." He had lots of talent but had become a very proud man. The missionaries had heavy hearts for him and the ministry he was charged to lead for the Lord.

Her African Family

As she prepared to go to the states for furlough, the interruptions were many as the Africans would come continually to sit with her. Literally hundreds came, and the packing had to take second place. Not only did they come to say goodbye, but to share problems and burdens. One pastor came to tell her that his wife didn't want to pray with him. Doris prayed with him and asked God to help him love his wife more anyway, and to keep praying that he would be a good husband and father. Naturally, many problems start with us, not the other guy.

Home for first furlough from Africa,
Christmas 1956

Departing from the field for furlough
on an MAF plane.

Furlough
and
Recoup

Furlough and Recuperation, 1973-74

Doris felt limp and ready for furlough after all of the events of the previous months. At this stage of the game, she would welcome an uneventful trip home without delays and schedule changes. To schedule a trip for furlough, one is already worn out trying to finish programs, packing, moving everything personal out of the house so that the next person can call it theirs, finishing up with writing special events programs, children's lessons, correcting and typing Bible school lessons, and most of all greeting and saying goodbye to the steady flow of the dear people who have come to say goodbye. "You are coming back to us, aren't you?"

"Mama, we know that you need a rest, but please don't abandon your children here."

"Where ever we are, in the gardens, on the road, fixing food we'll be praying for you."

"*Ani ndoye mo mingui na fade ani sambela mingui teti mo.*" (We love you very much and we'll pray much for you).

It was a two-day trip over bad and sometimes almost impassable roads to get to Bangui, the capital, for the first leg of the flight towards the United States. A flight schedule from a third world African country didn't always work out perfectly. In fact, it rarely did. One trip, she arrived in Paris about midnight, and found out that she had been bumped from the plane that was to take her to New York. Didn't God know how worn out and tired she was? The airline scheduled her to fly out the next day and put her up in a big expensive hotel on the Champs Elysees in Paris. Why the delay? A renowned United States basketball team needed all the places on the plane, thus the change of scheduling for Doris. But wait! That isn't the end of the story!

A special news report came out the next day, telling of a plane that had crashed over Great Britain on the way to the United States. Yes, it was confirmed that it was the same flight from which she had been bumped; the plane with the basketball team had crashed. No survivors! Once again, God let her know that He wasn't finished with her ministry for Him on this old earth. Her life was spared for many, many more years of service for a great and loving God.

After a deluxe breakfast at the hotel she headed for the airport for the flight to New York. This flight left as scheduled. After eight hours of flying she saw the Statue of Liberty from the window of the plane, and she knew she was approaching the United States. As she went through customs there, she was asked by the customs officer if he could buy one of the African paintings that she had in her baggage. She replied, "No, I don't bring things home to sell."

He answered, "Well you gave the right answer." Then she knew that it had been a trick question. The next step of the trip was a helicopter ride between airports, New York to New Jersey, from where she would get her plane for Elmira. She was informed there that she had just missed the plane for Elmira, New York. Like a zombie, with her two suitcases and hand luggage, she roamed around the airport until the next flight for Elmira was announced. Afraid that she would go to sleep and miss the next flight, she didn't dare sit down for very long. Although she arrived completely tired out, God reminded her again that He was the strength of her life (Psalm 27:1). She was glad that her God wasn't in her pocket, like that of one man seated beside her on the plane, who told her his god was, referring to his wallet.

As usual, it was good to see most of the family at the airport in spite of the lateness of the hour from of the delayed flight. Before she left Africa, she had brushed up her winter clothes and made some dresses. To top it off, she had borrowed a suit from another missionary so that she would look somewhat decent upon arrival. No one seemed impressed at her efforts to look chic. Nearly the first thing that the family exclaimed was, "She needs to go shopping for some clothes tomorrow." She was informed very soon that the clothes she had from four years ago before going to Africa just wouldn't pass now. But who was complaining? They all pitched in to buy her new ones.

What's New in the USA?

It wasn't the lack of modesty, nor the social drinking accepted by nearly everyone, nor the protesters: hippies, snippies, tippies, nor the poodle haircuts, or lack of them. *Newsweek* magazine had done a good job of clueing her in on the so-called new styles. However, she often mulled over in her mind a question that was asked of a pastor friend: "How many Christians in America really believe that Jesus is coming soon?"

"Surely not many," he answered, "or America would be quite different today." Just think what the answer would be today.

The following incident will likely cause a few chuckles. She was enjoying the cold weather and the snow back home, so her niece and nephew decided to take her on an excursion with the snowmobiles. As they traveled up Switchback Road, they hit a patch of ice hidden under a blanket of snow. Ginnie, her chauffeur, was horrified when Doris found herself under the sled rather than on top of it. There she lay with the machine on top of her, still running, bottom side up. She was laughing so hard at the situation, while Ginnie and Ronnie looked horrified, as if the Arctic Cat had attacked her. What had they done to their Auntie? They set the Panther right side up, freeing her from her newly acquired position. No harm done, except for the bruises that gave a bi-racial appearance in several places on her body. There weren't many if any offers to take her for a ride after that episode. It wasn't her fault, really. Well, I don't think it was.

Glad to Be an American

There were literally hundreds of hugs from God's own who had been praying for her through trials and joys for many years, many from the beginning of God's calling to her when she started Bible school in 1944. The opportunities and invitations came from across the United States to share what God had done for and through this little lady missionary. Ten weeks in camps and vacation Bible schools were a blessing to her heart, as she saw children and young people accept Christ. Repeatedly, while she was in the States in many different churches, young people who she had met in camp would come and ask her if she remembered them. It was such a joy to hear them tell of decisions made for Christ during camp, missionary meetings, or vacation Bible school. Of course, she didn't remember everyone, but it always brings back wonderful memories of the ministry He entrusted to her. That is just a little taste what is to come in Heaven.

Sitting in a restaurant near the Bible College, a young man came to her, pointing his finger at her and saying, "It's all your fault." Naturally, she wondered what she had done. He proceeded to tell her of one of the times that she had been the missionary speaker for vacation Bible school at his father's church. She had challenged him with the question, "What are you going to do with you life?" Due to that little wake-up call, he dedicated his life to serve the Lord as a missionary. He and his wife have been serving the Lord in Italy for many years. It doesn't stop there. Today, all four of their children and their families are missionaries in that land, too. What exciting business to serve God. He does the calling; we are called to be faithful ambassadors with a wonderful message.

A Journey of Faith and Service

The car doctors had already assured Doris that her nine-year-old Chevy with almost 100,000 miles on it could make the trip to the West Coast. She picked up Elda Lon on October 16th near Altoona, Pennsylvania, and they headed for the West Coast. They took the northern route to Chelan, Washington, speaking in churches, colleges, and schools, and visited family and friends in many of the towns and cities on their way. Doris didn't even have to use any of her knowledge of mechanics. Thanks to garages and filling stations, the little car kept running. A fuel pump needed to be replaced the very first day out, and Doris could hardly believe that it could be done in less than an hour. Remember, they waited for months for parts to arrive in Africa.

Two new snow tires in a wooden box her brother Claude had built for her were strapped to the roof. Another spare tire, curios, screen, projector and slides, two boxes of literature, and books written by one of her professors from Bible school all found a place in the trunk. That left their clothes, both for hot and cold weather, to go into the car someplace.

The snow tires developed bulges, but the next service station had two tires she could buy to replace them. The generator started clanging and screaming, but at the service station, a phone call made for a convenient and instant replacement. The air filter burned out, but that was replaced almost automatically. At 10:30 p.m. in Butte, Montana, they were able to have a headlight replaced immediately. She was reminded of the time in Africa when she had to change all of the rims on the truck to get tires to fit, and that had taken several weeks.

They hit a snowstorm in Stevens Gap, and how glad they were to have snow tires due to the loving foresight and advice of others. Wonders and scenes met their eyes as they traveled along and over mountains. Her greatest joy was the fellowship with God's people; how God blessed her heart to see how excited and up to date the dear ones were at Chelan, Montana. What better and more encouraging sign could one ask for? This was evidence that they had been reading her prayer letters and praying. How her heart was saddened as she sat in the office of another supporting church noticing that several packets of her prayer letters sent for distribution to the congregation lay unopened. Praising God, she believed that this was an exception and not the rule.

Western Bible College had invited her to share her burden for Africa with their students, and then they journeyed on to Hawthorne, Nevada to spend time with George and Alberta Meadows and the church folks where he was pastoring. Those dear ones merit mentioning, although everyone who was an encouragement in that ministry can't be named. The George Meadows family was in her home church when she was a teenager. Their lives were a blessing and example of real believers to this young girl down through the years. When the Lord called her to be a missionary, they were both on the front lines to cheer her on all the way. She was invited each time she was home from the field to share her ministry in each church where they ministered, as well as line up round robin conferences with other churches in the area. If she was anywhere near them in her travels, she would stop in for lunch, or at least for a prayer time together.

Such was the case once when her route took her near them on her way from northern Pennsylvania to a meeting in Maryland. She was driving a tired and retired model Chevrolet. When George asked if he could try it out, naturally, she gave him the keys. As she continued on down the road, she checked to see if she was going to need gas soon and discovered that he had filled the gas tank. This pastor and his wife have already been promoted to glory, and the church he last pastored in Hawthorne, Nevada continues to pray as well as contribute financially to Doris' support.

Early on the furlough trail, she was thrilled to be reminded of how He would take care of all of her needs. Dr. Lowe, who was one of her professors when she was in Bible school, had come to her home church for a weekend of special meetings. When the offering plates were passed the night before she left on a trip, she felt directed of the Lord to give all that she had in her wallet to the Lord. No, she didn't have any other funds for the trip, but she felt constrained to give all and trust Him for the next step. She can just hear some readers scornfully say, "That isn't even good planning." She said nothing to anyone about this step of faith.

She went home and prepared for her journey, which she was starting early the next morning. Sometime later in the evening, her brother Aubrey and his family drove in the driveway. He handed her a five-dollar bill, saying, "I forgot to give this to you for your trip when we were at the meeting this evening. We were well on our way home when the Lord reminded me, so as you can see, we turned around and came back." That was more than she had in her wallet when she had emptied it into the offering plate. At a church in Fallon, Nevada, a tire salesman there thought that her tires were too bald, so he replaced all of them. Her thrilled heart just kept on being blessed over and over as the Lord took care of every need, big and little, of this little single lady missionary. She just keeps on being excited about serving a wonderful God.

Condemned Without a Hearing, or "No Case"

This was the message that she received after leaving for furlough. How can this be? She already had her return visa. She could go back to the field of the Central African Republic, but would it be the greater part of wisdom? The Africans were repeatedly writing to tell her to be sure and come back. Should she write to the President of the Central African Republic himself? Some of her former co-workers were also praying. What was the best solution that would honor the Lord for the ministry there? She wept and sought His will, and many others on both continents were praying for the Lord's direction for her future ministry for Him. A poem that someone had penned helps explain the testimony of her heart through the trial:

"I know not but God knows
Oh blessed rest from fear,
All my unfolding days to Him are plain and clear.

Each anxious puzzled "Why?" from doubt of dread that grows.
Finds answers in this thought: I know not but He knows.

I cannot but God can: O balm from all my care!
The burden that I drop, His hand will lift and bear.

Though eagle pinions tire, I walk where once I ran
This is my strength to know: I cannot but God can."

Although the cries of "Miss, come back, please come back to us," were multiple from the dear African brothers and sisters, she knew that if God led otherwise, even if her heart was breaking, she must be an obedient servant of an Almighty God. If she went back, would it hinder more than help the ministry among the people that she loved so much? She was asked to consider the need in the Chad Republic. Bordering the north side of the Central African Republic, this too, was formerly part of the French Equatorial Africa before their independence from France. If she went there, she could use both the French and Sango languages. She did know that she would need to learn the Sara Madjingaye to be able to communicate with much of the population there.

The dear ones at Bangassou kept sending messages to encourage her to come back to them and the ministry there. "Thank-you miss for training such a good wife for me," wrote Pastor Kima who had married Djiambi, her adopted daughter.

Djiambi wrote, "Thank you, miss for teaching me all that I know so that I can be a good pastor's wife and teach others the good things that you taught me."

Mbombate, one of her first Bible school students wrote, "The chief enemy of our souls has planted much unrest among our people. You pray hard for us, won't you?"

Many dear ones were joining her in prayer, as she continued to seek God's direction and ask others dear ones to pray. She wrote in one of her prayer letters, "God is in control and there is no reason to develop an ulcer." Of course this is good advice for the other guy, isn't it? She prayed, as did many others. The Lord directed her and gave her peace to go to Chad. In her display, the map of Chad replaced the map of the Central African Republic as she presented the future field of ministry. Notwithstanding, nothing has ever replaced her love and burden for her dear African family in Central African Republic.

She continued to travel from coast to coast across the United States, encouraging God's children to pray with loving hearts for past and future ministries on the continent of Africa. It was one of the hardest periods of her life. Little did she know that it was only preparation and training for some even more difficult and troubled waters in her future. She could now sing as she wept, "Troubles almost 'whelm the soul; griefs like billows o'er me roll, tempters seek to lure astray; storms obscure the light of day; but in Christ I can be bold, I've an anchor that shall hold." ("My Anchor Holds," a hymn written during the 19th century by W.C. Martin). Her trials, heartaches, dangers, and sicknesses were minor events in comparison with the storms many saints and martyrs, through the centuries had experienced and lived through victoriously.

And So We Travel On

Doris felt led of the Lord to spend a few weeks in France on her way to the Chad Republic. She had been speaking and translating materials into Sango for several years and she had the joy of being on the field when the Sango Bible was finally in print in 1967. The delight was hers as she saw young and old hold the Word of God in their hands so lovingly, and in the Sango language for the first time. The excited amazement on their faces as they cried, "Merci Nzapa, merci Nzapa" (Thank you God, thank you God), is a picture that would never leave her memory.

Now she was going to another of France's former colonies where Sango was spoken less, but understood by many. Since God had permitted her to have extra studies in the French language, and more and more children in Chad had the privilege of being taught in French schools, she felt that a few weeks in perfecting the language would be profitable. In southern France, in view of the French Alps, she could study and rest. She was in great need of rest. She had enjoyed seeing so many prayer warriors as she traveled and reported to churches in the United States, but it had been extremely tiring as well. Among her most precious memories are the many dear, praying ones in these churches who really cared and prayed faithfully for God's ministry through her.

France, Here She Comes Again!

Packing barrels for Africa, plus taking care of all of the last-minute preparations to leave home again for four years was extremely fatiguing, as she was on her way again. This time she was headed to the Chad Republic, with a few weeks in southern France on her way. She enjoyed this time in France. Not only did she enjoy further studies of the French language, but also the exceptional view that she was blessed to enjoy from her window at the school. She had a direct and splendid view of Mont Blanc, which was really quite magnificent. She even visited some other areas of France that she had not gone to before when she was a student in Paris, due to lack of time and limited funds. A nice visit to Switzerland was the icing on the cake. All her life, God gave her so many hands-full of His blessings. She was continuing studies in the beautiful French language, and enjoying a very much-needed rest. Nevertheless, Africa was calling, and she was eager to arrive once again on African soil.

Chad

1972-73

Studying the Sara
Madjingaye language
in the village

A special offering for
Doris

Sleeping
accommodations
during the dry, hot
season

The pastors in Chad
receiving the New
Testament in the
Sara Madjingaye
language. Later
martyred for their
faith.

Missionaries
expelled from Chad,
November 1973.
(Doris is third from
right in red).

Chad Bound

Doris left for Chad in the early spring of 1972. Before leaving the ground in Paris, she met a young Chadian lady who was boarding the same plane with her two children on their way back home to Chad. Her husband was in Paris studying, and eventually would be returning home to become a customs officer. They traveled on a 1944 DC3, and by the time they made their first stop, the little one was cuddled up in Doris' arms.

They were supposed to arrive at Fort Archambault, (Sarh), at 6:30 a.m. This was one of those times that the calendar worked better than the watch. They stopped in the desert at Am-Timan to unload several pieces of freight and pick up two mail sacks. The tour there let them view several trucks loaded with khaki-clothed men. From there they were taken on what seemed like a safari, where they landed in amongst the giraffes, baboons, and lots of huge birds. Since it was a natural reserve, there were many waiting to hop the plane for the next stop—thirty-four people for twenty-nine seats. Despite arriving two days and three hours late, Mary Baker, Viola Brown, and several Bible school students were there at the airport to meet her.

Wilma Childs extended to Doris real loving hospitality in her home for over a month, as Doris waited to be settled into her own residence. Among many other tasks such as teaching and evangelizing, Wilma still found time to be a real blessing to Doris.

The climate in Chad was not the same as it was in the Central African Republic. It was hot and dry, bordering the Sahara desert; it was a different Africa. This was another adjustment for her after having lived nearly twenty years in the tropical forests to the south. The ministry was also different, but the message and the need were the same. She felt so blessed to be called to be a servant of Almighty God. There were needy people who needed to hear the message of God's love and how to have a new life in Christ, and many precious people who needed to know Jesus died for them.

The cries from the Central African Republic to the south kept coming even after Doris arrived in Chad: "They say that you are not coming back to us here, but the God in which you taught us to believe is greater than all, and we keep on talking to Him. Hurry back, we love you so much, mother of mine." This was written by one of the teenage boys, not that she needed letters to remind her of all of her spiritual children and grandchildren. God gave her perfect peace to go to Chad, but even then, she kept looking for the big moving day when He would tell her to come on home to heaven where all the redeemed will be together.

One More Language to Learn!

At the mission station, she could communicate in French, Sango and even English. She knew that she had to isolate herself to put another language under her belt. With her grass mat, tape recorder, some food staples, and boiled drinking water, she went to live at an outstation where, other than the pastor, only Sara was spoken. As usual, the Africans were very hospitable. The pastor and his family moved out of a tiny grass-roofed mud hut in order for her to move in. Her many guests patiently showed her different items, naming them repeatedly so that she could record and memorize them.

She learned the name for rats in an interesting fashion. The family had had a good catch of them the previous night, and they brought the fat ones as a gift to "Miss." How would she get out of this pickle? She needed much wisdom from the Lord to not offend, as they were being very sacrificial with their gift. You didn't get meat to eat every day. With many motions and waving of her hands, she told them that they needed the rats for their children. She did learn later that their meat was very similar to squirrels and other small game. They burned off their fields on purpose to catch the rats that ran from the fire. They were not dirty, gutter rats, and if they came from the fields of grain they were well fattened up. This was practiced in the Central African Republic as well, but she never needed to become personally involved.

Besides learning the language, she was exposed to many beneficial African manners and customs, which were a plus for her ministry among them. She especially loved cuddling those dear little African children who had learned that she loved them too, even if her black skin was all washed off (that was their explanation for pale white faces).

As soon as she was back at the mission station, she asked the Lord to help her be a blessing and a benefit to the ministry. Almost immediately, she was helping to run off reading lessons on the mimeograph, an important ministry. Sandy Banasik, a missionary linguist working with the Sara language at the Koumra station, had prepared these primers. Doris' part was to prepare the stencils, then duplicate them by use of the aged, groaning mimeograph machine which cried often for attention.

Most of the African adults had not had the luxury of going to school. The New Testament was soon to be translated and printed in their own language; the leaders and people were all eager to learn to read and to enjoy reading the Scriptures. Doris had reading classes for all ages, men and women, boys and girls. Only a small percentage of the children had the privilege of attending government schools taught in the French language. Chad too, had formerly been a French colony before independence. On Saturday, the missionaries attempted to help them learn to read in the tribal language. She learned as much from them as they did from her; they just learned faster.

When the New Testament in the Sara Madjingaye language was printed and ready for distribution, Doris would never forget the privilege and thrill of putting it in the hands of three of the oldest pastors. As they fondly held it in their hands, they wept and cried to God with thanksgiving, "Thank-you, God, thank-you, God." Needless to say, she too was weeping with them. It was a sight that she had seen before as the entire Bible in Sango was printed and held by thankful hearts and hands in the Central African Republic.

The above-mentioned pastors were some of the first who had learned the real meaning of God's grace. They had accepted Christ as their Savior many, many years previously. To have the Word of God in their language, in their hands was a real answer to prayer. Nothing has stayed in her memory with more delight and thankfulness than the glow she saw on their faces, as they tenderly wrapped their hands and hearts around that New Testament in their own language. She didn't contribute to that translation since she had recently come to Chad. It was a special blessing to her heart to know that the Testaments had arrived at Koumra on the same truck as her baggage. It was one of the many delights that the Lord gave her during the relatively short period of time that God allowed her to serve Him in that land.

On the Road Again

Road trips to the bush stations with Wilma in her International Scout held many new experiences, accompanied with much laughter at themselves. The Africans knew what they were doing, but those dumb American ladies were just learning the manners and customs of the people. At least they were trying. At one of the outstations, special living quarters had been set up just for them. The top and sides were constructed of woven mats. No doors were included in this special home, so they hung their wrap-around skirts at the doorway.

Of course, this was not very good protection against the wild animals roaming around, especially at night.

Doris made some trips by herself to have her Faithful Women conferences. Since Doris was one of the originators of this program in the Central African Republic, and had seen what a blessing it was continuing to be to the African women down country, she wanted the same blessing for the ladies in Chad. Then too, the pastors, having seen the success of the ministry among the women in Central Africa, were constantly begging her to have retreats for the women of their churches. Initially, she was responsible for the whole program until she could train leaders. The African pastors were very thankful to have these dear ladies who loved the Lord with servant's hands and caring hearts.

What Do We Do with the Second One?

A few years after Doris went to Chad to minister, she was in a Faithful Women's conference out in the bush, when she was called to the hut next door to deliver twins. The first baby was immediately put into the mother's arms, but when the second child was born they put him aside to die. Much superstition presided among the older women of the village, and they were sure that they would be cursed if they let the second baby live. The mother, a much younger woman, was not allowed to make any decision about the situation. Needless to say, Doris immediately resuscitated the child, cleaned him up, clothed him, and put him in the mother's arms. The father, a born-again Christian, returned to the village after a day of hunting, and heard the story as the older women accused Doris of saving the second baby, thus putting a curse on their household. He came to Doris and thanked her over and over again for saving the child. She told him that God had timed it all. How often was she in that outstation village? Maybe once a year. But God used that to open blind eyes as he said in Acts 26:18, "To open their eyes and turn them from darkness to light, and from the power of Satan unto God, that they may receive forgiveness of sins and inheritance among them which are sanctified by faith."

She was still in the village for a few more days to finish the conference and both babies were doing fine. She couldn't help but have a heavy heart for the many hundreds of babies in that land who were meeting the same end because of unbelief and superstition. Oh, how badly they needed to hear and know God's Word, which was all the more reason it was worth having these women's conferences to share the word of God and guidelines for godly living.

Initially, she had all the classes from dawn to dark. That is why God had sent her with His message to these needy people. It was worth all the fatigue and heartache to eventually see changed lives. Little by little, some of them, especially pastor's wives, who had learned to read, could take over some of the classes. Doris would take her little old accordion to classes to teach music. They loved to sing, and Doris enjoyed hearing their voices raised in a joyful noise to the Lord, pecking out the notes on the accordion to be able to have quartets of four-part harmony for both men and women. "I can't, but He can," was her cry as she continued to help them make beautiful vocal music.

Her literacy class on the other side of Koumra was quite a challenge, but also a blessing. Usually, about twenty-five women attended and really labored over learning to read the Sara language. Teaching others to read a language that she didn't know well was quite a challenge for her. The women would giggle and say, "She sees it with her eyes, but she can't talk it. We talk it, but our eyes don't see it." The women patiently tried, and one after another they would yell, "I see it, and I speak it." This could be the work of many months, but the success was blessed. Most of these ladies had little or no formal schooling. One day David, a student from Northeastern Bible College, went with Doris to the literacy class. As they retuned to the village he said, "Do you really think that the lady I was trying to teach today will every really learn to read?" Many, by God's grace learned to read. Sara Madjingaye was the most difficult of all of the languages Doris had studied, and discouragement often came when she couldn't communicate. With so much to do and so little time, the Adamic nature would get impatient and cry out *when?*

Baggage is Here

Doris' baggage had finally arrived. Of the five barrels, rolled bandages, sample medicines, baby layettes, and children's clothes made up four of them. One crate in the shipment was a Lazy-Boy recliner rocker that had been completely paid for with green stamps. The number of books of stamps it required was unknown, but they were collected from churches east and west, north and south. All across the United States, God's own, dear loving people knew that she could use the stamps, so they collected a sufficient amount to buy the recliner. One by one, the missionaries assured her that they needed to try it out to make sure that it would be comfortable enough for Doris. They even used it for an extra bed when they ran out of guest beds.

While in the States, many doctors and medical personnel had given Doris a lot of sample drugs; she was busy getting all separated and classed before sending them to the medical clinic (hospital) that was on their station, as well as to the outstation clinics. Dr. Dave Seymour had established a medical work on the Koumra station, which involved equipped medical personnel. During two to three hours in the morning they also did surgery. Ruth Carlson was a midwife and nurse. Lorraine McDowell called herself "Dr. Killemoff," worm specialist, or lab technician. Along with African students who also made up the medical personnel, Doc's wife, Ruthie, not only ministered at the hospital, but also had a big ministry in showing hospitality. There were always lots of guests on mission stations. Even the people who were just trekking through Africa had all the mission stations scoped out in advance.

The electricity was generated by diesel engine and had to be turned on during the time for surgeries, so Doris decided to wire her house for electricity. Since the motor was on only in the daytime, she installed a battery charger that charged up while the light plant was going during the day to make her twelve-volt electrical system useful at night. The system of wiring was rather crude, with extension cords running from one end of the house to the other with a few connections to plug in to. The lights weren't exceedingly bright but they were much cooler than the kerosene lamps or candles. It was good that it didn't have to pass inspection, as it is certain that no electrician would have been impressed. Not many non-electricians were impressed either. "La-dee-da!" It sort of worked, anyway!

The cows, goats, and sheep that ran all over the place, including the verandas, didn't increase her patience. The recently planted garden, although it had excellent sandy soil and a fence, soon had nothing left but a few blades of corn. Part of the fence was stolen, and the cows reached over the existing fence since they were hungry, too.

Repeatedly through the years of ministry in other lands, concerned churches, family, and friends would inquire about her needs. Now, she was in Chad. In one of her prayer letters her answer was as follows: "Faith to trust Him more, His grace and love in living to exalt my Savior, not me, and His long suffering to understand and bear the frustrations."

Storm Clouds Overhead

Little by little, the African Christians, as well as the missionaries, became aware that the enemy was creating unrest in their midst.

President Tombalbaye, with a listening ear, was becoming more influenced by the philosophies of their closest neighbor to the north, the Libyan president, Kaddafi, who made repeated trips down to Chad, even to some of the bush villages where Doris met both presidents. As to Kaddafi, there was no doubt in any one's heart and mind as to his position concerning the Christians.

President Tombalbaye professed to be a Christian. He had even once been a leader and teacher in one of the churches founded by Baptist Mid-Missions. There was no change in the message or work of the missionaries, but the violent revival of ancient customs had placed the missionaries and the Christians of Chad under terrible and tragic attack. The unrest became more and more pronounced, and the old ritual of circumcision which had been abandoned years before for the most part, was one of the tools Satan used to stir up the country and try to stop any teachings from God's Word.

The African Christians tried to be very cautious in their conversations and reactions to the many changes. Many of the Christian teenage boys, whose uncles and other family members were insisting that they go through the tribal rites, came cautiously to the missionaries, asking them to help them hide from these family members. Although many of them had Christian parents who objected to the initiation, there were other members of the family, such as uncles and grandfathers who lived by these tribal rites and were forcing them, even to the point of kidnapping, to make them participate. Many of the older people who had gone through the process before they became Christians knew how diabolic the whole process was, and although sworn to secrecy, they strongly advised the young men against taking part. The African leaders and pastors advised the missionaries to not be involved in any way. There were many prayer meetings and special intercession was made for these precious young people.

Even though much of the time the atmosphere was quite tense during this time, a sense of humor helped much as they pushed forward in the ministry that the Lord had given them to accomplish. The following is from one of Doris' prayer letters sent to the States about her car, with its customary need for repairs and parts: "Did you ever fasten a piece of plastic hose to the side of an engine because it was giving off too many undesirable fumes? Now I have two exhaust pipes coming out of the back of the little car accompanied by lots of fumes. My little car has been running like a top, but I was told that it needed a motor overhaul. So pistons, rings, gaskets, valves, and the like have been ordered. Don't they sound like exciting presents to tie up with a red ribbon for Christmas gifts?"

Doris would occasionally take Dr. Dave's truck, at his request, to run the ambulance service for someone who was ill at one of the outstations. On one of these occasions, as she was traveling down the road, a human barricade of young boys going through the initiation rites hindered any further progress of the journey. First, they asked for money; Doris had learned not to carry any with her. "Then give us your headscarf," they said. The lady missionaries made it a practice to wear a headscarf, as was the African custom for church services. Doris replied, "I had planned to attend prayer meeting with the people before returning, but if I give you my scarf, I'll not be able to do so, will I?" Recognizing this vital part of their culture, the boys broke rank to allow her to continue on her way. It was evident that at least some of them knew that it was important for her to follow this custom.

The rest of the trip went without a hitch; however, this was not the end of the story. The initiates carried out this practice as part of the protocol of the revival of cultural customs. Anyone on nearly all of the roads heading out of Koumra could experience being stopped at one time or another. It was an inconvenience, but no one was injured in any way. Many were the prayers that went up asking God for wisdom and direction that comes only from Him, seeking the best way to help these people know the love and peace that comes only by turning to Christ for salvation.

It was called a cultural revolution, and surely, the desire of many Chadians was to revert back to their own cultural customs that existed before colonialism. Many of these customs identified them as a race, but, sorry to say, paganism existed, and the initiation rites were far from being God-honoring practices. The Chadian Christians, because of their acceptance of Christ and the teaching of God's Word, refused to return to the old rituals of worshiping idols. One of the pastors declared that no one could force him to return to "praying to the big stick," referring to trees and inanimate objects. The Christians in Chad could not, and would not comply with the demands of the government, which would result in betraying Christ.

The return of the ancient initiation rites brought the past to life again, which included old-style executions of those who resisted those rites. As was mentioned before, the missionaries tried to be very careful in what they said or did. The message they had brought to Chad was the reason many of the Chadians refused the old ways. It was hard for some to understand that it was Christ, not the white man's customs that had changed the hearts and lives of those Chadians who had accepted God's way to live. With the same devotion and tenacity as the Christians down through the centuries, they were horrified at the thought of betraying the Lord Jesus, even if it meant death, which was for many the case. The positive side of returning to the initiation rites was the rebuilding of tribal skills and national pride. Notwithstanding, the pagan worship and practices were so contrary to the preaching of the Bible that born-again Christians learned quickly to resist the pagan rites encouraged in the devil bush.

One of visits Doris made to an outstation village gave her much sorrow. One of the men of the village had died. They were all gathered in the middle of the village square going through all of the pagan ceremonies. Over to the side of the village, the widow was tied up to a tree. When Doris inquired as to the reason, the chief told her that the widow would be buried alive with her husband's body, so they had tied her up to prohibit her from running away.

Yet another bush trip to a village found her in the midst of a mob that was burying alive one of the deacons of the church. They had dug a hole big enough for his standing body. Part of the ceremony was to force all the villagers, including the Christians, to dance and sing around the burial site. Naturally, her heart hurt for them all, even those who were forcing this type of ceremony. They knew nothing of Christ's love and compassion for each one of them. How badly they needed to know of the compassion and love of an Almighty God.

Missionaries became the subjects of many false accusations. They were accused of signing and circulating a petition against the Chadian Cultural Revolution. No petition ever existed, and no missionary personally participated in any of these widespread allegations. From every standpoint, the situation was hard and heart sickening for them, missionaries and Africans alike. The Chadian leaders had requested that the missionaries refrain from even speaking about what the population was facing. Their hearts hurt so as one by one, the young people would come in the night and request to be sheltered. The missionaries lived through the people's heartaches with them, which resulted in many sleepless nights as they prayed for their dear African family facing this time of tribulation.

The older pastors who had themselves experienced the horrors of the initiation rites before the gospel came to their land were especially sought out. One of the Chadian pastors who Doris knew when he attended the seminary in the Central African Republic came to her and asked her to take him to Sarh, a town about one hour away from Koumra. She told him that she'd gladly take him, but she didn't want to know why he needed to go there. Later in the day, after spending several hours there in Sarh, he said, "Miss, I have business here, and I'll not be returning with you today."

Without fail, when she returned to Koumra she was asked about him: "He told me that he would return later," was her answer. Her heart told her that he was fleeing south to the Central African Republic.

The next day, he was at her door: "I was going to flee, but I just couldn't let my Chadian brothers go through these trials alone."

One by one, the Chadian pastors were imprisoned, including the one mentioned above. There were many scare and panic tactics used to influence the people, and especially the young men and boys, "If you don't willingly go for the initiation, we'll take you to prison," was their threat. More and more fear was implanted in hearts. Churches and all classes were closed. The decree came through the villages that no one could sing or pray in their homes. Imagine a law against praying in your own home. They didn't stop praying. Their law didn't include the missionaries' homes, thus many of the young people had good times praying and praising the Lord together. Even then, if there was a spy in the midst, the young people were reported and often arrested.

The missionaries attempted to be very careful as they shared God's promises from His Word to refrain from saying anything against the new laws and lawmakers. The class for the French school kids Doris was teaching during their noon hour was the only class that they determined wasn't against their new laws. Every day she traveled to the school in town to teach the lessons that had taken many hours to prepare. They were very attentive as they listened to the truths that helped them understand what a gracious God had prepared for them. Not one boy student missed those voluntary classes. There was unspoken hurry to grasp as much as they could in a short period of time. Maybe tomorrow Miss wouldn't have the freedom to come and teach them from God's Word. Because of their work at home, the girls were unable to stay for the noon classes.

Granted, the missionaries were aware of some of the persecution and hardships that the Africans were experiencing, but they didn't have the slightest hint that they themselves would soon be ordered to leave the country. In retrospect, they probably didn't want to believe that it could happen to them. When the order came for all missionaries, except medical personnel, to leave Chad, they had less than twenty-four hours warning. Much of the remaining few hours was spent, at least at Doris' house, in all night praying and singing hymns of praise. What was in store for their dear Chadian brothers and sisters? As they left the station the next morning on their way to Sarh, they all were convinced that they would be back in a few weeks. At that time, their concern was more for their African brothers and sisters than for themselves. The missionaries were under house arrest for a couple of days at Sarh as they waited for the government to send a plane to take them from that land and the people to whom God had called them. They took very little baggage with them. Doris even forgot her camera that was sitting on the dining room table.

One of the missionary nurses had loaned a suit to Doris, as she wasn't equipped for winter weather. When she arrived home, her brother would tell her that it was pretty shabby, but it was warmer than any other piece of clothing she had. Going through Paris and New York at the end of November, she was more concerned with being warm than being classy.

Finally, the small Chadian plane came to Sarh to take them to Djamena on November 29, 1973. Miraculously, they were able to book flights to the United States and Europe. The image of Israel, an African leader who worked with the medical team at Koumra, rests engraved on Doris' heart and mind. There he was, the one and only African who had dared to come to the airfield to see the missionaries off to their journey. He was Dr. Dave's right hand man, and was killed shortly after on a trip he took for Dr. Dave to the coast.

After the missionaries had left the country they heard that the thirteen pastors who had been imprisoned were later buried alive, as were many of the other Christians who refused to compromise. The pastor who had come to Doris for help when he had intended to flee to the Central African Republic was among those martyred. It takes a great deal of courage to be a martyr, but these men knew Christ and were true to the cause of Christ right to the end.

The missionaries had no bodily injuries; none the less, it is impossible to put into words the grievous condition of this demoralized group as the plane carried them away from this beloved land and cherished people—so many beautiful people—mothers, fathers, sons, and daughters forced to become candidates in the next initiation rites.

Arriving back in the United States just before Christmas, the joy of being with family and dear friends was dimmed by the heartaches and burdens they carried for their dear family in Chad. Communications were almost non-existent. Any news received was hastily shared with the others. They had to keep believing: "When the enemy shall come in like a flood, the Spirit of the Lord shall lift up a standard against him" (Isaiah 59:19). Doris' sad heart was encouraged and gladdened as she traveled from coast to coast, as so many of God's children reminded her that they were caring and praying for God's dear ones in Chad. The initiation rites scheduled for December, the month after the missionaries were expelled, were rescheduled for January. Needless to say, they all rejoiced in the way God answered prayer in delaying these rites.

They wrote from Chad, "Tell the Christians to keep praying. Our hope is in the Eternal God. He is our portion in spite of harassments and persecutions here."

"Never will we take part in an adulterous religion. So we die. That's alright too."

"Pray that we will never forget the greatness of our God. We thank God that your blood was not spilt here and for the Word of God you missionaries planted in our hearts."

"Physically we are well but our hearts continually bleed. Sometimes in despair but in spite of the threats and sufferings we know that we are not forsaken by our God."

Why Baptist Mid-Missions Only?

Baptist Mid-Missions missionaries were especially selected for the persecution by the Chadian government because they taught the people to conform strictly to the teaching of God's Word. It is probable that other missions in the area were not forced to voice their convictions. Baptist Mid-Missions was working in President Tombalbaye's tribe and his home area, and supposedly, the issue there was more accentuated. The idea of integrating some of the old heathen ways mixed in with the new was not acceptable. To embrace some of the old customs, which included worshipping of Satan and related practices, just didn't wed with the teaching of God's Holy Bible. Of course, the Chadians were much more aware of old heathen ways than were the missionaries.

False accusations abounded, such as stating that the missionaries were circulating petitions that criticized the government. It was soon evident that there were some disgruntled people who caused many of the trials experienced by the mission and the Chadian Christians. The missionaries didn't necessarily hear of all the trouble that was stirring. For the sake of Christians and leaders, they listened to the warnings of their dear African Christians leaders to not even whisper criticisms. The African believers' own steadfast Christian principles prohibited them from submitting to the humiliating demands of paganism. At that time, the government was not threatening the missionaries as to what they could or could not do. Their greatest suffering was seeing their brothers and sisters in Christ being persecuted, including an order to have no more gatherings to hear the preaching of God's Word or to pray together. With heavy hearts, the missionaries carried the burden with their African brothers and sisters for counsel and direction for the future.

Where to Now?

The first general Baptist Mid-Missions conference after being expelled from Chad was in Jamestown, New York in March of 1974. Nearly all of the missionaries from Chad were at the conference, including the medical personnel that had remained on the field when the rest had to leave. Due to the unrest that continued in Chad, the medical missionaries who had remained in Chad were now evacuated and were present at the conference. The unrest had continued. It was the general consensus of the mission that a complete evacuation of the rest of the missionaries would be a wise decision.

Imagine all of these missionaries together, each one waiting on the Lord for His answer to the question, "Where to now, Lord?" Four months had passed, and the situation seemingly had not improved. For a bit of added excitement, Doris got the attention of the group when she developed a bad case of malaria during the conference: "Aren't missionaries noted for bringing souvenirs home from the field?" she commented.

France

1974-93

Student retreat in the Pyrenees, representing around a dozen countries

"Help!" Doris stuck in the barbed wire fence at one of the retreats in the Pyrenees.

Student gathering at Doris' house after church and lunch: "Can you find me?" (Center)

The Baptist church in Bordeaux.

The gang from the kitchen to end of the living room. Always room for one more.

I was a guest of Suhail's family from Jordan as he defended his doctoral thesis.

Dr. Dan defending his thesis. After he finished he gave each member of the jury a Bible.

Doris made the dress for the wedding of Ando and Lala, both doctors, and devout Christians who work in the church at Bordeaux

Doris made the dress for Pauline and Dan's wedding long distance with no pattern, just measurements. The bride was in Mauritius and Doris was in France.

Newlyweds in a field of lavender.

And So We Journey On: Campus Bible Fellowship in France

Most of their tortured tears dried, and the missionaries squared their shoulders to the continuing challenge of Christ's commission. God doesn't close one door without opening another one. It was apparent that re-entry into Chad wasn't in the near future. Nevertheless, they could continue to pray and care for the suffering Christians in Chad even as they looked to Him for their next field of service. "I, being in the way the Lord led me," was Doris' testimony as she shared how He was leading her to start a Campus work in France. "Go," was the order from the Lord, and that she did!

If the Chadians had gotten as far as university in their schooling, it was natural for them to go to France to continue their studies, since French was the official language in Chad, and it had previously been a French colony. Doris was heading to France to start a ministry among university students. This fact of course helped her decide to launch the campus ministry there: "impossible for her, but not for God."

French Study Again

Although she had previously studied the French language at the Sorbonne, the Alliance Française in Paris, and the French Language School in Albertville, France, and had a variety of diplomas to prove it, she had been ministering in the Sango and Sara Madjingaye languages in Africa, and thus spoke in several languages all at the same time. A good name for it would be "stew." So, back to language school again she needed to go if she anticipated ministering among university students. They called the course "Perfecting the French."

To the Uttermost Parts of the World

Of the group who had been "invited to leave" Chad by force, one couple and one single lady headed to France to work in the local church-planting ministry. One couple went to Ivory Coast. One felt called to work with Campus Bible Fellowship in the States. One spent years in children's ministries, teaching, writing and publishing material for children's work translated in other languages. All of these changes in their lives and ministries were some of the ways God sent them out to the regions beyond. One and all patiently waited for news of their dear family in Chad with the desire to see the door open for them to return.

None of them had wanted to leave Chad and the dear people there, but God was sending them to the uttermost parts of the world to tell the same wonderful message of God's love to many other nationalities across the globe. Doesn't that sound like the commission given to God's children in Acts, Chapter 1? Our God is great and He directed their steps and burdened their hearts to their next field of service. The challenge alone, given by God to these pilgrims, was hard to imagine, but they knew that there was plenty to do. So with a burden for many souls around the world, they followed God's order to go to the ends of the earth.

In nearly twenty years of ministering to the university students alone, Doris saw over eighty countries hear the gospel message. That might not have been the case if they hadn't gone through the tragic heartache of their expulsion from Chad. Missionaries couldn't go to all of those countries, but students from those countries came to them through their university studies in Bordeaux, France. At the university, she made some very fruitful contacts among the students from many countries. Some even made the trek by train to Sunday services at the church in Savigny: students from Germany, the Islands, Tanzania, the Central African Republic, etc. Only heaven will give the exact count of those that gave their lives to the Lord Jesus during that time of their ministry there.

During the time she was in the Paris area, she lived in the apartment over the Baptist church in Savigny, which was a good distance from the center of Paris. The missionaries who normally resided at this apartment were in the States on furlough. The building had been recently built and still had several unusable parts. For instance, the heating system was one in name only. Naturally, it was all good missionary training. To go to her classes each day, she ran to catch the train, made connections with the subway and ran the last seven minutes, out of breath to sit for five hours of class each day.

Thanksgiving in Paris

While living in the Paris area, they enjoyed introducing the good old American holiday of Thanksgiving to about twenty students who came from varied countries, and were studying French with them. With a good Thanksgiving dinner, they were able to share the message of the gospel and explain the real meaning of the holiday. Among the subjects of discussion were, "You don't really believe that there is a real devil, do you?" The Spanish students let everyone know that it wasn't true that there were many martyred during the Inquisition as heretics if they didn't become Catholics. Naturally, there were multiple nationalities with lots of opinions. Many were the questions discussed in our French classes, a foreign language for all of them. They had a very good teacher and lots of discussions in class. The teacher and many of the students were infidels; nevertheless, they loved to discuss different issues. One advantage was that the students had a right to differ, and they were not graded on their political and religious differences. All of this was in God's program of preparation for the ministry awaiting Doris among university students, especially in Bordeaux.

Bordeaux: So Little in Her Hands

The missionaries on the field decided to start the campus work in Bordeaux. This was mainly due to the placement of the church near the center of town. Also, there was a nucleus of students already attending the church there in town.

All of the missionaries that had to leave Chad were unable to take any goods with them. Materially, they pretty much had to start over, even to have a bed to sleep on. Thus Doris slept on an air mattress on the floor in a room without windows, located up over the room where the church had its meetings. The accommodations, although rather frugal, were offered to her at very little rental cost. In a very short time some of her missionary co-workers found a folding bed they could spare for her. Having spent many years in Africa doing bush work with just a mat on the ground for a bed, she didn't have too much of a problem adapting to so little. Her many years in Africa, as well as being brought up during the Depression, helped tremendously in adjusting to the meager provisions as they were graciously offered. Money was scarce, so it meant learning to go with the flow. She had answered God's call to minister to university students, most of whom also had very little of this world's goods.

Dan Lacey, one of Doris' co-workers, had a 16mm movie projector, which he lovingly used to show films for campus ministry. They rented Moody films and proceeded to have a showing every two weeks. Being led of the Lord, Doris stood before the Director of Student Affairs at the University. She said, "We would like permission to let the students know about the films and other events that our campus ministry offers them without cost." He assured her that there would be no problem, and gave her full liberty to publicize all of the campus activities that were free. Little did they imagine how profitable that permission would turn out to be. This led to many deep knee bends as they put flyers under the doors of all the residents, had Bible stands at campus restaurants, and placed posters on all the bulletin boards inside and outside of the buildings because of this officially granted permission. Every time a cleaning lady or some other worker would tell them that they couldn't be there they just said, "But we have *carte blanche* (blanket permission) from the director." No one had computers to do their work at that time, thus the posters, flyers, tracts, with Snoopy as their mascot, and other invitations and publicity were typed and run off on the good old mimeograph machine.

Exciting Times Ahead

Almost immediately after the first distribution, Doris received the following letter from a student: "On arriving at the residence a few days ago, I discovered a crumpled flyer in the waste basket, and on it was your address. I am lonely. I cry for hours. I find myself lost in the midst of a crowd. Help Me!" Within thirty minutes, Doris was on campus and at Myreille's door. Doris assured her that the flyer with the invitation to a film was real, and that they would all be glad for her to accept the invitation.

Doris became like a second mother to Myreille. A few weeks later, due to a need for lodging, she came to live with Doris for several weeks. A few years later, after Doris came to Florida, Myreille and her husband made a trip to the States to visit her. At the writing of this book, almost forty years later, Myreille and her husband are still in contact with her. The lovely packages full of French goodies they always send for birthdays and Christmas are always a reminder that they haven't forgotten her. The most exciting part of the story is that she and her husband are faithfully living God-honoring lives and still calling Doris "Mama."

On Monday evenings, almost immediately, the Bible study and discussion groups led by Dan Lacey started in the Sunday school room. University students have lots of questions, and the French students loved to voice their opinions. All of this kept Dan on his toes as he led the group. There was a nice group of varied nationalities, saved and unsaved that came, and they didn't even serve refreshments. Many of them were attending faithfully the other activities of the church. The meeting place where church met for several years wasn't very big, and the room was packed on Sunday morning. For a long time, the church looked in vain for something to buy or rent. Not only was it small, but it was located in the red zone of the city with a brothel next door.

Many were the days that she would go out, around the corner, to stand in the crowds before the restaurant and weep. The opportunities were numerous, and the multitude of students presented an impossible task. She learned quickly that she couldn't, but her Lord could. She had to lean hard on His arms. What did she have to fear or dread; blessed peace with her Lord so near; "Leaning on the everlasting arms."

After sixteen months, Doris was able to rent an apartment located close to the university restaurant where ten thousand students enjoyed their noon meal each day. The moving day wasn't a big hassle, as the only thing that she needed a truck for was a refrigerator she had bought, and a freezer on loan from the Lacey's while they were at home on furlough. Doris decided that the missionary expression, "Blessed be nothing" would apply quite well, since she had so little of material goods to move.

She thought she was finally living in the lap of luxury. In her new apartment she had a living room, bedroom, kitchen, and bathroom. She needed to heat the kitchen with the oven. Gas heaters in the bedroom and living room, and warm water in the shower stall took care of those rooms.

The young people had already helped to establish a Bible stand at the exit of the university restaurant where they offered Bibles and tracts to one and all. This was also a convenient place to distribute flyers and invitations to their activities. Many from various countries stopped to talk, discuss, argue, and listen. Since she lived so near, if they were interested in continuing to talk, she would invite them to her place for a snack or tea.

Since her apartment was close to the "La Place de la Victoire" (Victory Place), which was near the market place, it was also conveniently located for the winos and the drug addicts. Several times a day there were visitors at the door asking for food or money. She would open the front door a wee crack and hand out a cup of coffee, as well as cookies or bread, if she had some on hand. Knowing that many hundreds of faithful, praying folks were concerned for her and the ministry God had entrusted to her, she asked for continued wisdom as to when she could safely open the door fully and invite them in to talk and serve snacks.

Cookies, coffee, or bread always accompanied a word about the love of Jesus for them. If she had something to give, she didn't hesitate to give it. Was her generosity misused? Naturally! She suggested to a couple of winos who had been coming to her door daily for two to three months that they go down to the market and unload trucks at 4 a.m. for grocery money. They continued to come to her door, and then it was with lots of excuses about why they couldn't go to work: "My back hurts me."

"I didn't wake up in time to go to work."

"No one at the market needed help," (Ha!), and so forth.

God reminded Doris that by giving to them all the time, she wasn't really helping them learn to stand on their own two feet: "Tomorrow is the last day that I can give you anything to eat, so you must go look for a job. So many others are hungry and needy, too." You guessed it! They were at her door the next morning right on time: "No, I can't give you food today or any other day," she said.

"But Miss, we are very hungry. There are no jobs."

God had led her to do her homework, and she said, "I checked with the merchants at the market located less than ten minutes away from my place, and they said that they could use help anytime." It was hard to turn them away, but she knew that God was leading her to do this.

On Sunday, as always, she had fixed dinner for all of the students who had attended church and had time to come. Other young people came to lunch as well, if they desired. On Sundays, the students were used to the downstairs door being left unlocked so that they could come on up to the apartment. As a rule, the door upstairs to her apartment was kept locked. Doris opened the door for a latecomer, and in walked the two winos as well. Most of the students were already at the table set up for twenty to twenty-five people. The winos started to threaten Doris in the hall that led to the living and dining room. Immediately, the sound of chairs being pushed away from the table was heard and the hall way was full of students rushing on the double to Doris' defense. Their stunned, alcohol-controlled minds realized that Doris' God was protecting her once again. However, before they left her home the students witnessed to them. It wasn't wise to mix them with the new students who had joined them for dinner for the first time. They heard the gospel once more and were reminded of the time of services at the church.

Prayer meeting was the first service after that event. Yep! The men arrived at prayer meeting, but in a very drunken state. One of them had a sharp dagger type knife in his hand, which they tossed back and forth. Each time that they would throw the knife into the new carpet, they kept promising Doris that the next one was coming her way. Charles Anderson, a missionary who was leading the meeting, suggested that they all start praying for the requests. The winos, being filled with alcohol, got a bit distracted with that statement, and with the others' heads bowed, ready to pray, Charles said, "As it is getting late, Doris, would you take Mme. Destieux home?" She was the only other lady present. This incident was used of the Lord to burden their hearts to pray and care more for a lost and sin-sick people. They had pity and concern, and were asking the Lord how they could safely win them to Christ. Their condition was the result of having no knowledge of the gospel according to God's Word. Each one present could say in their hearts, "There but for the grace of God, go I." It wasn't just the ones who had become slaves to alcohol or drugs that needed to know of Jesus love for them.

Bible Stand

One day while at the Bible stand at the restaurant, a young lady named Isabelle stopped to talk and look over the printed material on display. She assured Doris that she was a Christian because she had been baptized as an infant. "Who is Jesus to you?" was the question that Doris asked her. She hesitated in answering and then went on her way. When Isabelle got back to her room she asked herself why that lady had asked her that question. She needed to have an answer to give her, so she dug out the Bible that her former boy friend had given to her and tried to find an answer. God sent her to them at the stand several times. As the student retreat, which was to be in the Pyrenees, was approaching, Doris asked Isabelle if she'd like to go along. Instantly and firmly she said, "No, I am not interested."

Student Retreat in the Pyrenees

One of the avenues God used in a great way for the ministry among the University students was the annual spring retreat in the Pyrenees Mountains. Charles Anderson, who was especially fond of mountain hikes, strongly encouraged Doris to see about the organizing of a retreat for the students. If you haven't read his book,

"Beyond My Limits," his trek on the trail, I can highly recommend it. The promise of skiing, the hikes, and the fellowship was used in a big way to encourage even the non-Christians to attend, which brought great rewards for the Lord. Several found the joys of knowing the Lord Jesus as their Savior while attending. Bible studies, discussions, fellowship, music, and fun were all part of the program.

Late evening, the night before the departure for the Spring Retreat, Isabelle called Doris and asked her if it was too late to go along. Doris told her to pack, and assured her that they would find room for her in one of the vehicles. The departure was to be at 6 a.m. After all, they just had to throw another bag on top of the car and squeeze in another passenger. No car seats needed as they didn't shift around much in spite of the turns and twists traveling up the mountainside to the shelter that they had rented.

Mr. Fouchier, a retired French army colonel, was the speaker. Isabelle bombarded him with questions that he patiently answered. He, being French, could better help than an American with an accent. The mind of a Frenchman doesn't necessarily accept quickly that salvation is a free gift from God. They have to reason things out. Isabelle went back to Bordeaux as a born-again Christian. She was still having doubts about the security of everlasting life until she learned that when God said "Everlasting," that is what He meant.

One year, Dan Lacey, one of the missionaries, came down from Caen, where he had moved with his family, to speak at the retreat, and brought some students with him. Among them was Jamel, a Muslim boy from Morocco. Eventually, Jamel accepted the Lord, graduated from Bible school, and became the pastor of the church where Dan had been ministering at Caen.

God gave Doris the idea of having them comment on the pros and cons in a notebook. Brigitte wrote, "Glory to God for the riches of His Word."

Luc from Madagascar wrote "Together we have made the fellowship God-honoring, in spite of rainy weather." Brigitte and Luc later married; he became a customs officer on the island of La Réunion, a department of France on the Indian Ocean. Doris later met their lovely children in Mauritius.

Jacques, a young Frenchman, called Doris to find out the times of services at the church. The person in Paris who had led him to the Lord had encouraged him to call Doris when he moved to Bordeaux. He called and started attending services immediately. His work didn't allow him to attend all the services. With a hunger to know more of God's word and His plan for his life, he would come every afternoon to read the Scriptures and pray with Doris at her home. As a new Christian, he had come to Bordeaux to work as a cook in a high-class restaurant down town. In a short time, he was able to change jobs, which gave him more liberty to help in God's work. He began studies with Charles, and later was trained to be the pastor's assistant.

Wedding Dresses

University students, more often than not, would be looking across the aisle at the opposite sex. Discussion groups often followed the Sunday dinners, and many would stay for game time. Retreats helped the students to get acquainted with each other. "Fun and Film" nights also helped things along.

Doris added sewing wedding dresses to her list of occupations. Martine was the first one to need one. The missionaries first became acquainted with her at the student restaurant. She let them know in no uncertain terms that she wasn't interested in their tracts or message. As adamant as she was against the message, surprisingly, she decided to read one of the tracts that she hadn't destroyed, "God's Word Gives Light." Lots of questions followed, and very shortly she saw her need of a Savior. As fervent as she had been against the gospel, God changed her heart and she became fully dedicated to announcing the gospel message to others.

Pascal was in the French military and had accepted Christ as his Savior through the ministry of the Savigny church, where Doris had become acquainted with him when she was studying French in the Paris area. When Doris changed apartments, there was much painting and repairs needed. Pascal and Mr. Fouchier came from the church in Paris to help Doris make the apartment more livable. Pascal had the opportunity to meet Martine there, and the rest is history.

Martine wanted Doris to make her wedding dress, as she didn't like the styles or the prices in the store. Imagine running competition with the French seamstress! She didn't think that they were very worried about the competition that she might bring. Martine was a lovely young lady with a desirable figure, but she wasn't interested in showing a lot of bare skin. Since she knew what she wanted, she drew Doris a picture. Doris prayed a lot and made the dress to the best of her ability.

Creative Prayer Letters

Doris' prayer letters sometimes entertained the folks back home as she recounted some of the challenges of living in France:

"The following is the car talking to give an idea why the little Renault 6 was so busy. International transport for Taxi, van, trucking, train, bus station, campus, church, schools, conferences, retreats, excursions, job hunting, grocery shopping, and garage—ouch, that hurts; gas station - that hurts, too. Portuguese, Hatian, Ivorian, Camerounese, Nepalese, Vietnamese, Martiniquian, Guadeloupian, French, American, English, Ghanian, Zairois, Central African Republican, Chadian, German, Congolese, Syrian, Lebanese, Venezuelan, Spanish, etc.

"Susie Renault will now speak her piece about traveling (Doris' first car in France).

'I feed on a very expensive liquid diet. I'm not really worth very much on the market, but I still work and work, and it would cost a lot to replace me. Doris was quite embarrassed with me, as she tried to remove the front tire to change it. She has changed literally hundreds of tires, but this one had a nut that wouldn't loosen even though two students came by to help with their muscles. Even the garage had a struggle to get the nut to co-operate and operate.

"Doris lives on a very busy street. The student restaurant is just around the corner. The students park all over and very close. Sidewalks, driveways, etc. are all considered parking spaces. I have a few waves and crimps because of it. Nothing serious. The parking is done by sound, not by sight. With cars parked on the sidewalks on both sides, it makes for quite an art to try and weave between. Sometimes Doris has a problem trying to get in the front door of the apartment building. Frequently, it is necessary to walk the bumpers of the vehicles to get to the door to enter her apartment.

"It is extremely tight parallel parking by sound. I really hurt from getting all those bumps trying to get into that little space. I have acquired an increased number of dents and rattles. Someone just knocked out a headlight in the process of parking a car. I need new shock absorbers real soon, before we take the scheduled trips to Paris and the Pyrenees Mountains within the next month. Doris doesn't misuse me, but she uses me a lot.

"Arthur wants to share his thoughts too. You might think that Arthur is a strange name for a gas range: 'After nearly four years of getting along with a wee little gas burner, Doris was able to purchase me. My full name is Arthur Martin. Wow! Is she ever a slave driver! She helps some, but I sure don't know how she could manage all these meals that she makes for the students without me. She really had a puzzle to solve when the gas company turned off the gas. She came home the other night and smoke was coming out of a window that she thought was hers. The street was full of trucks, policemen and firemen. One fireman escorted her to her apartment and checked the walls of the apartments next door. Both apartments next to hers were furnishing the blaze. There I sat as pretty as ever, but no gas meant no fire and no heat. Doris panicked a bit because she needed to fix a meal for four people.

"Really, I was going to tell you how hard I work. It wasn't to tell you of my few rare moments of rest. You already know about her Sunday dinners with big groups of people each week. I have an automatic oven, which helps tremendously. The food is prepared and put into my oven, and then I labor while she goes to church. I even tell time and shut off automatically if she doesn't forget to do her part and set my buttons. She has a huge rice cooker that helps out a lot. Most everyone likes rice, which is a big help in making the meal stretch for that gang of kids. Even when there is no food to fix, I often stay on to heat the kitchen since central heating is not furnished in our mansion.

"With all of the extra work needed on the new (old) building in need of a facelift on the program, the volunteer workers need to go full speed. One man came from Toulouse a couple of times to spend a week each time to help, and most of his meals were taken at Doris' restaurant. Extra meals mean extra work for me. To help complete the face-lift for our building, a group of five came down from the Paris churches for a week. Several from the Bordeaux area joined them, making a party of eight to ten daily. Doris and I did our part by using our talent to keep their stomachs full and happy. After all, we are in France. Shouldn't we prepare special meals for our guests? Teamwork is the answer. Do you remember that I said that she is a slave driver? In spite of all that, we work pretty well together most of the time.

"When Doris went back to the States for her father's funeral, Eunice Dark who was living with her had no problem working with me. You see how versatile and co-operative I can be? In fact I co-operate with everyone that has a desire or whim to cook something.

Doris and I are glad that the gas was off but a short time, thus we can keep in the culinary business together for the glory of the Lord. Many of the students come from other countries and nationalities where rice is a main dish, and they are well schooled on how to help out making sauces, and stir-fries to complete the meal. Some of them even came on Saturdays to give me work to do; they need my oven for most of the preferred desserts. Thanks to all of you who helped Doris buy me so that I could change residence and be in business for God. I'll stop chatting now so that her boots can share how they suffered walking miles on Doris' feet.'"

Her Boots Speak, too.

"As the story goes, the Covington Baptist Church ladies' group wrote to ask Doris if she had a specific need. She told them that they didn't sell boots big enough for her feet in France. So the ladies shopped and found us. We are just the right size, length, and width, and in just a few days we arrived in France. We go up and down lots of steps, streets, and sidewalks, seven days a week. When we aren't in the shop for repairs (new heels twice, soles replaced once, two new zippers) we are putting in kilometers of travel time. In spite of the cracks and wrinkles we have developed, we are still good for several more miles. She decided that she didn't like the color so she dyed us. It might have helped some. Down the streets, up the stairs, down the hallways, and to the hospital we go.

"Doris knows that our time on this earth is limited. We are going to wear out, but the message she is sharing is eternal. Two days ago, this letter was going to be written, but Samuel came by with a troubled heart, and two and a half hours later he accepted Jesus as his Savior. He went away rejoicing in his newfound faith in Christ. Two girls arrived shortly after his departure and Doris talked with them for three hours. Christian then came with his cousin Patrick, who said after hearing the message of God's love that Patrick would be a thief if he hadn't told him God's message. He promised to read the tract that she gave him.

Paula and Candide's mom died, a trip to their house to give comfort was in order, then on to the hospital to do some visiting with the sick before we went back home so that we could get a little rest. Next, we ran to the post office to get stamps to mail this letter to all of you folks who pray for her. Doris insists that we can't slow down because Jesus is coming very soon, and there is so little time to do so much. I think if we wear out before she does that she'll just buy some more boots and keep on running."

At Last, the Church Had a Building

With hearts full of praise to God, the Baptist Church was installed in its newly remodeled building in December of 1979. The building had formerly been a cabaret in the red light section of Bordeaux. Many were the willing hearts and hands the Lord used to help get the building converted to a place of worship to Almighty God. Some of the students were a big help, and God's servants from other places in France helped in many ways as well.

For example, Fred, a fourth year architectural student, humbly sacrificed much time to help reconstruct the building. Knowledgeable in the construction business, he literally spent hours by himself, plugging away, restoring a kitchen, classrooms, and so forth. He wanted no recognition for his labor of love. The work on this old nightclub would soon turn this stronghold of Satan into a local Baptist church. God's children had a sincere desire in their hearts to exalt the Lord, together with a burden for others who needed to know the joy of the Lord.

A Work in Progress

The missionaries had Bible stands at the university restaurants where they shared testimonies, and distributed tracts and copies of the Gospels. Not only did they have stands at the restaurants in the city, they also had the liberty to set up Bible stands on the university campus. There were many curious students who came by with questions, discussions, and arguments, in spite of opposition to the outreach, like a sign on the side of a building that said, "Ten dollars to one Jesus isn't coming back again." Ironically someone wrote under it, "I take that bet." This was only one of many expressions of opposition to try and discourage the message of God's grace.

Marie and Marguerite were two of the most dependable and faithful co-workers to run the stand from the beginning. Many others had the burden and joy of sharing Christ as they handed out tracts and flyers at the exit of the university restaurant. They learned early that the students didn't stop for discussion when they were rushing to eat. The Bible stands were one of the most progressive means of sharing the gospel.

Saïd, a muslim, once he discovered the stand, would always look for the team and stop by the stand to discuss and talk. After about three years of meeting and eating with the gang on a regular basis, he decided that he needed to open their eyes to the truth that Jesus wasn't God. Regarding Doris, who he appreciated, probably because of a perpetual open door to talk and eat, he said, "That dear lady needs to hear the truth, and I shall convince her today that Islam's teaching is the true way." That same afternoon, after sharing God's Word with him for three hours, he accepted God's Son as his Savior. This was after about three years of being exposed to the Word, by the testimonies of God's children, the ministry of the retreats, and other student activities to which he attended faithfully. He is now working in a hospital as a cardiologist.

Zuheir, a muslim from Syria, was also contacted at the Bible stand and witnessed to by God's people for two and a half years before he made a decision to live for Christ. He then went to Bible School in France and now lives in the United States. He heard the message of God's grace and followed the Christian walk for awhile. Many were the people that prayed for him before and after a seeming decision to accept Christ.

Doris did an individual Bible study each week with each new convert and other babes in Christ. Many were the tears that she shed over those who didn't want to take the time, or were just plainly not interested to hear about the Savior. Besides the many Sunday dinners, individual Bible studies and discussion groups, films, plays, and musicals were all part of the programs that were offered to the students. Regardless of the nationality or color, they really enjoyed each other and the fun of being together like one big happy family. Most of them loved to sing, and many enjoyed playing games; the food was a big improvement over cafeteria grub, and chiefly, they just all enjoyed being together. Sunday dinners needed to feed between fifteen to thirty kids; regardless of the number they shared and shared alike. All the regular ones knew they had the liberty to invite any new comers to Sunday dinner, or even those they contacted at the restaurant. One young man to whom Marie witnessed decided to come to Doris' house for lunch with the girls. When he entered the apartment he made the announcement that he didn't like Americans. Doris signaled to the others to let him talk awhile. Can you imagine his surprise upon finding out that Doris came from the United States?

Christmas at Doris' House

Once the Christmas gang all arrived and were seated, they were so crowded together that they were fixed in place for the evening. Imagine them crawling over one another when an urgent need presented itself; Doris got a few giggles out of their calisthenics.

On Sunday evenings after the discussion time, singing together, and then some good competitive game playing, they slowly and hesitantly said good-bye to return to their lonely rooms on campus. Many were from other countries and cities. They made up their own family together at Doris' house. She would like to share some of the comments made by many with thankful hearts:

"Thank you for this home away from home where we can come and fellowship with each other as we learn more about our Savior and His Word."

"Thank you for being a mother to us all. You always have time to listen to our problems and show us that you care."

"It's not easy to go back to the lonely room on campus."

"Your home is a real home away from home for all of us. Thank you for your love and care."

"We all call you 'Mom' because you care. Your godly, caring counsel manifests your loving heart. You join in our grief and our joys as you cry with us and laughingly rejoice with us."

Apprenticeship Program

Shortly after going to France, Doris became the hostess for Kathy McEwen, the first of many college kids who came from the United States for a short missions trip. The following year, and for several years afterwards, Doris was hostess for many college students who came to minister in France for a few weeks in the summers. Her accommodations were far from being luxurious, without even a spare bedroom to offer them. For a few weeks each summer, she usually had a couple of girls who slept on the couch in her living room. Her one and only bedroom was rather small and equipped with a single bed.

The telephone rang in the middle of the night. It was a call from Ben Kendrick from the home office: "Doris, I have a wonderful couple who wants to come to France on the apprentice program, and I immediately thought of you as you have a history of being such a good hostess for these kids that may become future missionaries." In amazement she replied, "Ben, did you forget that I already have promised to take two girls this summer?" He answered, "Doris, you have had many years in the third world, and I'm sure that you can figure lodging for them somehow. Please don't say 'no' as this is such a promising couple, and you are just the best person to host them." If you know her, you know that Doris finally said "yes."

Now, for the rest of the story. The lady in the downstairs apartment just happened to buy her own place and was moving out just before the guests were to arrive. Doris checked with the owner of the apartments, with whom she had a good relationship, and was able to rent that apartment for her guests. Doris found someone to loan her a double bed the duration of their stay, and they were in business, as they could eat and live pretty much upstairs with the rest of the gang. This couple, Sid and Andrea Baker, of all those she had hosted, came back to France as missionaries. Ironic, isn't it? Not really. She calls it "God-directed." Some of the others did go on to serve the Lord as missionaries in other fields.

She hosted at least twenty-five young people from the apprentice program. Some knew a little French; some knew none. Some, but not all, knew how to peel potatoes. Most of them were trained to use dishwashers, but not all trained to wash dishes. Many down to earth chores had to be learned, but they all wanted to evangelize and win souls. It was a blessed experience for all of them both in the Bordeaux area, as well as the Evangelism Camp across the country of France.

Evangelism Camp

Each summer an evangelism camp was organized and hosted in one of the areas in France where Baptist Mid-Missions was planting a church. Christians came from other areas to help contact people with the gospel of Christ. The huge tent, which served as a place where every one could meet together to eat, have Bible studies, sing, or chat, was erected at a camp grounds surrounded with smaller tents for sleeping. Like the other missionaries, Doris' tent slept six.

Besides eating, they had Bible studies and lots of music by all. Every day, groups would go out to hold Bible clubs in areas around the cities. Some would be on the tract distribution team, and a follow-up team would contact those who showed interest. Everyone was busy in one way or another. Doris often found herself counseling or comforting a lonely camper when she wasn't helping with the cooking or out with a team.

God graciously worked through a group of thirty young people, plus missionaries serving the Lord in France. They literally reached people from all over the world with the gospel. Some of the teams were at the huge train station in Bordeaux, as many from different nations arrived and left. The beach was always a drawing card, offering a place of enjoyment for the campers. The Atlantic coast also presented an opportunity to evangelize a huge mission field. People of many nationalities accepted the gospel tracts that told them of Jesus' love as they were offered to them. Not only were they ministering to many nationalities, but also the young people who were sharing the message of salvation were Portuguese, French, Africans, Lebanese and Americans. During one camp alone, over two thousand tracts were distributed, many personal discussions were held, several addresses were given to them, and there were professions of faith.

A lonely soldier was out on the streets of Bordeaux where they went as a group to evangelize, even though the weather was rainy and cold, and they were all shivering. Naturally, it wasn't ideal to be on the streets of Bordeaux. They could have reasoned that no one would be out in that kind of weather. Their contacts were few; however, an audience of one listened as they shared the gospel message. René, a lonely and homesick soldier without a place to go, listened and accepted the message that went to his heart that same evening. Thus was born again a soldier for Jesus Christ. This lesson to be faithful and steadfast was impressed upon the whole group. The practical and impressive meaning of I Cor.15:58, "Therefore, my beloved brethren, be ye steadfast, unmovable, always abounding in the work of the Lord, forasmuch as ye know that your labor is not in vain in the Lord."

Testimonies

The following was a testimony of Jenny, one of the girls who was very timid and alone: "Other than my parents, you were the first person that influenced my spiritual life. Because of your kindness and true testimony, I said to myself, I want to be like Doris. I began to seek a closer relationship with God, and that changed my life. Your caring heart influenced my way of actions and love for my own children. This was in 1978, and the next year you took responsibility for me and my twin sister, making it possible for us to go to the camp in Caen. It was at that camp that I knew that God was calling me to serve Him full-time."

After preparing for the ministry, she and her husband, who she met at the camp, have served the Lord full-time in planting churches in France. Another part of their ministry was raising a family of five children to love and to serve the Lord as well.

Annemarie from Germany wrote, "Nancy introduced me to you in 1975. You told me that it was important to have a personal relationship with Jesus. I had never heard this before, even though I was a member of a Protestant church in my country. You introduced me to a missionary who spoke German, and she explained to me how to be born again. Shortly after that, I went to the evangelism camp, and there were many American students present (I am still in contact with a couple of them), and I shared a tent with Doris and Nancy. When I married, my husband and I helped start a new work for the Lord in Germany."

Because of her close relationships with several of the medical students, Doris was invited to visit the country of Jordan. Little did she realize the special treats the Lord had for her by ministering to college-aged young people who had come from many countries in the world to study in France. She flew into Amman airport where she was met by Suhail and Walid, who were both studying medicine in France. Thanks to them and their families, she did a tour of Jerash, Jabash-Gilead to the north; she traveled on a donkey into the city of Petra to the south, Mt. Nebo with its beautiful mosaic floors figured among other attractions, the Dead Sea to the west, where she took a little walk in the water, and Aqaba and the Red Sea to the south. Then, by special permission from key politicians, she went across the Jordan River to Jerusalem, Bethlehem, and other special places in Israel. Normally, she would not have been allowed to re-enter Jordan from Israel. By God's grace she was able to tour more of the Middle East in one trip than most tourists.

At another time, a trip to Morocco was arranged so that she could go visit the families of some of her kids in that country. Saïd was often in Doris' home and became another one of her sons. Saïd and his wife had made a trip to the United States with Doris, thus it was their turn to proudly have this missionary in their home and country. He was a student in France for several years, and then returned to his country of Morocco to practice medicine. Any time that any one was having a medical problem at her house, she would call him, and he would be there in five minutes. During a visit from her brother Floyd and his wife Ida, with Claudette and Tom, their daughter and her husband, Floyd became quite ill. Saïd was there in no time flat to minister to his need. Some of the family felt that without that quick doctoring they might have lost Floyd. God in His wonderful timing and provision used Saïd to meet an urgent need once again.

One of the couples that had lived with Doris for a few weeks, and had been students in France was getting married in Guadeloupe, and the Lord permitted her to attend their wedding. At the same time she was able to go back to neighboring Martinique, her first pioneer mission field, which was also was in the Caribbean. Many of God's family there were as happy as she was to meet together again.

After retirement, she had the joy of going to Mauritius, an island in the Indian Ocean, to attend the wedding of Annick, one of her girls who studied in Bordeaux. Annick had previously visited the United States with Doris. The Lord has allowed Doris to return to France to minister and see her kids and their kids and other ones dear to her heart. During her last visit to Bordeaux, they held a big celebration for her eighty-eighth birthday. Dear ones from all of the three churches, plus some from Paris and other places joined in the celebration.

How many weddings has she attended? How many weddings was she in the position of the mother for both the bride and groom? How many wedding dresses did she make? The dress for Pauline from Mauritius was made without a pattern or having ever seen the bride to be. She did have her measurements. Dan, her fiancé who was now a doctor, wanted a dress made by Mama Doris and had bought all of the material and trim to have it made so that he could take it back to Mauritius with him. I'm sure that the dress had to have some adjustments before the wedding. Dan had to return to France alone after their wedding, as they had to wait several months more for her to get a visa to come to France. She also baked numerous wedding cakes. They weren't professional, but she did her best, and it filled the bill. Marc, from Martinique, studying at the university, was very adept at decorating cakes, so that was a big help on that score.

Many were the times she went to the local market to buy flowers for weddings to decorate the church for their weddings. As college students and many of them working on their doctorates in different fields of studies requiring several years, their funds were limited. Most of them didn't even have a car. Doris was the taxi driver to take Lala and Ando to the motel after their wedding. She returned the next day to take them to the plane. When they returned from their trip her taxi was there to pick them up and take them to their new home.

Family and neighbors supplied the wedding pictures when finances didn't permit professional photography. One couple who was married in southeast France had their wedding pictures taken while standing in a field of lavender. Not many have that exquisite setting for pictures of their special day. Thus have been the varied circumstances and settings for not only pictures, but customs of the people in various areas of the globe where the Lord placed her to work for Him.

Jacques and Isabelle had been brought into God's family by the Holy Spirit and God's faithful witness for Christ; the third church that was started in the Bordeaux area met in their home for several years until the crowd outgrew the space. In a recent letter from Jacques, he shared how after the assembly rented for a period of a few years, they were able to buy and modernize a building where they had their first meeting January, 2013. Calvary love brought Jacques then Isabelle to Christ. They have five children who are all born again and serving Him. Yes, they are French.

Petra, Jordan, 1985

Tomb, Jerusalem

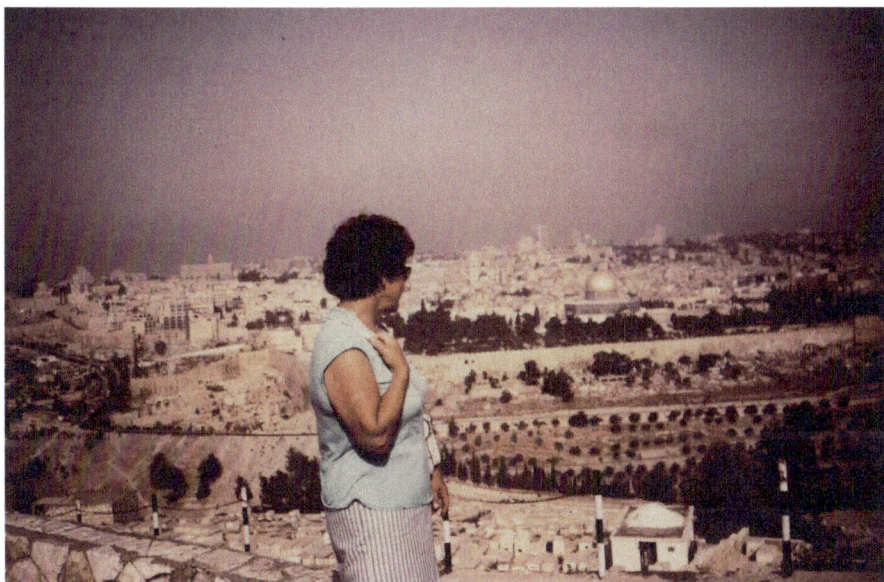

Looking over the city of Jerusalem

Epilogue

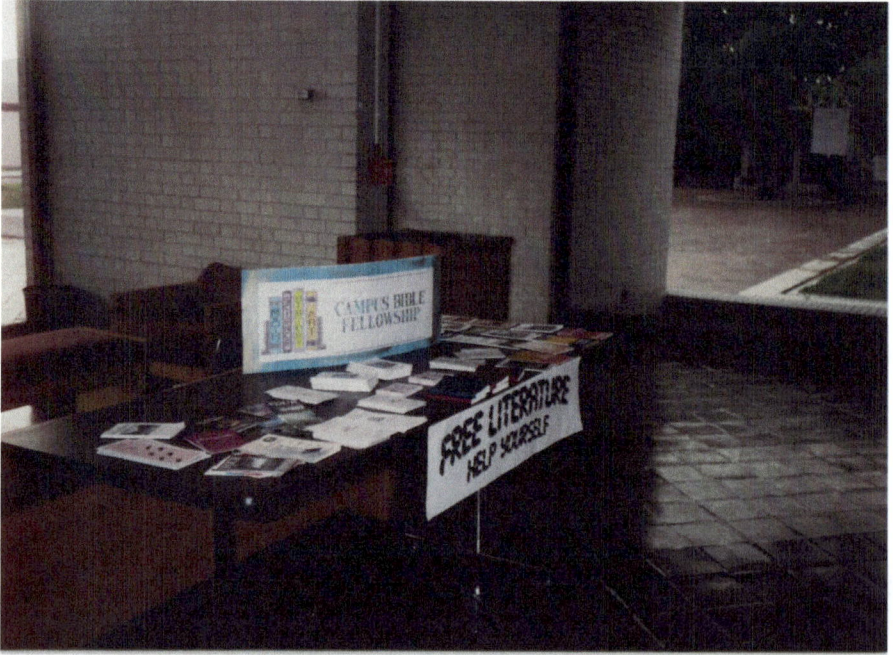

Bible stand at a university in Sarasota, FL

With former students from Bordeaux, Patricia, Therese, Pauline at Annick's wedding on Mauritius Island

As retirement time approached, I didn't know where the Lord would open a place to live for those remaining years ahead. Although I had no retirement funds, I relied on the Lord to supply for this need, too. God had graciously granted my desire to be where I could continue to serve Him. He had promised that He would supply all of my needs. I've never lived in luxury, but I never went to bed hungry, either.

In 1980, Anthony Rossi, the founder of Tropicana orange juice company, was led of the Lord to build Bradenton Missionary Village especially for missionaries without funds for retirement. In 1993, the Lord opened up a home for me at the Village for a five months furlough from the ministry in France. Even before returning to France, I applied for permanent residence at Bradenton Missionary Village upon retirement at the end of the year, and I was granted a lovely home at the Village, where I have been living since I retired. It is exciting to serve a Great God and He has allowed me to continue to serve Him in many ways, even in retirement.

Evangel Baptist Church: New Ending

Even during the five months that I was in the States reporting to churches, before I went back to France to get ready to retire, the desire of my heart was to tell a lost world that Jesus cares. Due to a burden for the Bradenton/Sarasota area, Art and Harriette Christmann had contacted Continental Baptist Mission to check on the possibility of starting a new church in the area. This was all happening at the time I was retiring from the work in France. Imagine my excitement to see how God had open doors for me to share in this challenge to minister for His glory. David and Mary McClintock and Bill and Terri Jenkins, missionaries with CBM, were excited about another wide-open and new mission field.

I became one of this group of Christian brothers and sisters who had begun to meet together to pray and look to the Lord for His direction. I was quite excited about having Bible stands at the university, since I had seen in France how affective and successful that ministry had been. We were able to (get permission) meet the requirements to set up a Bible and literature stand there, and our dedicated young people were quite enthused to help with this outreach program. Together, our vision for the lost encouraged us to do Bible Clubs, calling in homes, and special activities for the women, which included other groups from churches across the state of Florida. The Awana program was begun due to a burden that Brian and Debbie Pruett had for the youth. It quickly became a very effective tool because of the concern and burdened hearts of many gifted leaders.

Due to the dedicated effort of missionary builders, and the co-operation of many of our own congregation, our new lovely building was completed and ready for occupancy in the spring of 2003. From 2004 to 2008, Brent and Kim Hockema blessed our hearts with their loving ministry before journeying on to another place of service. As a replacement pastor for one year, Ray Mitchell challenged our hearts with God's Word, and many are the ones who have voiced the fact that he was used of the Lord to help awaken a burden for missions. Andy and Amy Goad came to us in 2009 and they continue to bless our hearts and share the burdens in our midst with their loving ministry for Him. Besides the local church ministries, which included helping and caring for others in their needs, even when I have felt tired and weak, God has always given me added strength to serve in one way or another, for which I have always been so grateful.

A Journey of Faith and Service

In 1996, God allowed me to have the joy to minister and share the gospel at the Olympics in Atlanta for seventeen days. Also, He has granted me several extra trips back to France and to my loving family there. I'm Mama to many, Grandma and Auntie to others, and all because of the message of Calvary. There is so much more that I could share of His loving care and happy opportunities as a servant for His glory. My heart is filled with praise for all of the prayer warriors who cared enough to faithfully intercede in every effort that was allowed me to win souls to a saving knowledge of my Savior Jesus Christ. As I journey on from one mission field to another, the desire of my heart is to be found faithful, with continued gratefulness for the high and holy calling granted to me by Almighty God.

My home and my neighbors